HOW TO
~~SMASH THE PATRIARCHY~~
MAKE THE MATRIARCHY

THE POWER AND PROMISE OF PRIORITIZING WOMEN

MAUREEN DEVINE-AHL

NEW DEGREE PRESS

HOW TO ~~SMASH THE PATRIARCHY~~ MAKE THE MATRIARCHY
The Power and Promise of Prioritizing Women

ISBN   978-1-63676-607-2 *Paperback*
         978-1-63676-270-8 *Kindle Ebook*
         978-1-63676-271-5 *Ebook*

HOW TO
~~SMASH THE~~
~~PATRIARCHY~~
MAKE THE MATRIARCHY

THE POWER AND PROMISE OF
PRIORITIZING WOMEN

Read +
change the world!

Maureen

Kira+

Change the world!

Mama

Table of Contents

To Elizabeth

May this all be ancient history by the time you read it.

Author's Note

I turned in the completed manuscript for this book on Wednesday, November 25, 2020. This, as many of you know, was just eighteen days after Joe Biden and Kamala Harris declared victory in the presidential election, cementing Harris as the first female, first Black, and first South Asian vice president-elect in the United States.

The timing of your book is epic, a girlfriend had texted me on the sunny Saturday afternoon of the Biden/Harris news. *I hope so! I honestly feel like I could keep writing and writing,* I replied.

Harris's achievement is monumental and should absolutely be celebrated as such. As should the work of all the changemakers who mobilized voters to make it happen. But when the announcement was made, I found myself only cautiously excited. I know now that while electing our first female vice president is an important step in the right direction, this progress is not finite, nor is Harris's achievement representative of access to equality for all. History proves progress can easily be reversed, and there is much work to do to ensure *all* women have the opportunity to thrive and achieve their dreams.

That said, it was shortly after this weekend I finally cemented the subtitle for this book. Previous versions included *How the Power of Inclusion Can Save Humanity*, and *How Empowering Women Empowers Humanity*, and, frankly, a few others. I came to choose *The Power and*

Promise of Prioritizing Women because I know now, without a doubt, that when women are better represented in leadership, progress tends to accelerate for all of humanity. So, yes, this is a book for all genders, about the power of inclusion, and empowering women. But, at the end of the day, what I found myself terribly excited about in the Biden/Harris news was the promise a first female vice president holds, especially when coupled with the largest number of women elected to congress. I know now it's important we all become comfortable with prioritizing the inclusion of women more fully, equally, and equitably, because humanity stands to gain so much when we do.

While my timing may be epic, as you read on, I invite you to remember my stories and research are but a snapshot in time, and we all have the power and responsibility to keep writing, learning, and changing the world.

With gratitude,
Maureen

Introduction

———

"If you don't like the way the world is, you change it. You have an obligation to change it. You just do it one step at a time."

—MARIAN WRIGHT EDELMAN, FOUNDER AND PRESIDENT EMERITA OF THE CHILDREN'S DEFENSE FUND; GRADUATE OF SPELMAN COLLEGE AND YALE LAW SCHOOL; AND, IN 1965, BECAME THE FIRST BLACK WOMAN ADMITTED TO THE MISSISSIPPI BAR. SHE HAS BEEN AN ADVOCATE FOR DISADVANTAGED AMERICANS FOR HER ENTIRE PROFESSIONAL LIFE.

Imagine going to your next book club meeting and learning the majority of attendees believe women:

- shouldn't be president;
- shouldn't earn more than men;
- shouldn't go to grad school;
- shouldn't have the right to govern their own bodies; and
- deserve the occasional open-handed smack from their husbands.

Maybe you'd quit that book club. Except, outside book club awaits a world in which 90 percent of the population is biased against women in politics, economics, education, violence, and reproductive rights. Men are regarded as supreme political leaders and business executives, despite clear evidence of their misplaced self-confidence, arrogance, greed, missteps, lack of empathy, and corruption. A significant portion of the population finds it acceptable for a husband to beat his wife. Ninety percent of countries have restrictive laws against women.[1]

Forget quitting book club. Time to build a bunker.

This isn't the start of a dystopian fiction novel. Instead, the above represents the very real findings of the first gender social norm index released by the UN Development Programme on March 5, 2020. Analyzing data from seventy-five countries who, collectively, represent more than 80 percent of the global population, the study found that 90 percent of the world's population harbors bias against women. Specifically, nine out of ten men and eight out of ten women hold at least one bias against women. Remarkably, only in six countries *on the planet* did a majority of people not hold a bias against women (Andorra, Australia, the Netherlands, New Zealand, Norway, and Sweden).[2]

I was about three months into my writing journey when these findings were published. Reading them marked one of many moments when a project that began with naive curiosity evolved to feel more pressing, serious, and urgent.

At the end of 2019, I decided to challenge myself to write a book, inspired by the advice I had received to *research and write about what you need to read.* I've always felt

---

1   "Report reveals nearly 90 percent of all people have 'a deeply ingrained bias' against women," UN News, March 5, 2020.

2   "Tackling Social Norms: A game changer for gender inequalities," Human Development Perspectives, United Nations Development Programs, March 5, 2020; Liz Ford, "Nine out of ten people found to be biased against women," The Guardian, March 5, 2020.

called to the work of empowering and uplifting other women in pursuit of equality. I was curious whether I was doing enough, if I could be doing more, and if I would live to see gender equality achieved in my lifetime. I wondered, What remaining barriers are there to achieving gender equality? What will it take to eradicate all remaining forms of inequality and inequity? Is achieving gender equality even the right goal? Will women ever just be able to enjoy life without everyday oppression? I was talking these curiosities over with a girlfriend at lunch one day when she said, "I know. Smash the patriarchy, right?"

Except the battle cry of "smash the patriarchy" was something I could never fully find my place in. Sure, in theory I'm on board, but I couldn't help but notice the phrase was often accompanied by clenched fists and bearing of the teeth (my lunch companion had banged her fist on the table). To me, the phrase invoked anger and discontent, surfaced embers of a smoldering rage, and played straight into angry feminist stereotypes. And it kept that stupid thing, *the patriarchy,* crossing our lips.

When I set my sights on smashing the patriarchy, it felt too much like war. Like something we must win. Something that is potentially unwinnable. After all, the patriarchy has been alive and well for about ten thousand years. If we declare war on the patriarchy, it presumes there will be winners and losers in the end. As a goal-oriented person, I know there are stretch goals and there are over-stretched goals. The former can be a great motivator. The latter can be a motivation killer. For me, smashing the patriarchy seemed an overstretched and ill-defined goal.

What happens after we smash the patriarchy? Can the patriarchy be fully smashed? Does the goal of smashing it mean women win? Men lose? Something else? What exactly does life look like on the other side? Even if we can smash this thing that has literally survived, well, *everything*, what is left in its wake?

As polarized as society is these days, I simply couldn't find myself in the rage of the movement. I feel strongly that if we're to recognize our shared humanity and build a healthy society, we owe it to each other to find ways of planning and communicating where no one is made to feel like winners or losers. Rather, we need to come together, identify what we need to work on, and focus on *building, growing, and making*; not *suppressing, defeating, or smashing*. In short, I want to ignore the damn patriarchy and make the mother-loving matriarchy.

I said something similar to my lunch companion that day. When I did, she leaned in, wide-eyed, and said, "Yes. That. How do we do *that?*"

That's where "make the matriarchy" was born. It started out a simple enough moment of alliteration. But, as you'll see in the pages that follow, I begin by researching existing or reemerging matriarchies around the world and find they are on to some pretty inspiring things. Matriarchal societies have a completely different power structure that is more inclusive, more creative, and often more prosperous for all. While these matriarchies have their flaws, no doubt, it is the roots of their power structure— the power of inclusion instead of power over others— that are, I believe, the same roots we need to channel in the creation of something new.

To be clear, this is not a book about matriarchies. It is a book about gender equality, the barriers that remain to achieving it, and what we stand to gain once we do. Together, we'll look around the world and look for lessons about progress and the power of inclusion. Matriarchal societies of the past and present are just one of those lessons.

As I collected lessons, I came to see each as a piece of a puzzle. I felt if I could find and connect the right pieces, perhaps a clearer picture of how we build a more gender-equal world would emerge. I learned from places with both encouraging and cautionary tales. Like Switzerland, where it took until 1971 to guarantee women the right to vote, then just forty-nine years later ranks as one of the best places globally for women's safety, security, and equality.[3] Or, the surprising global front-runner for parliamentary representation by women, Rwanda, where the 55.7 percent of seats held by women blows some of the most developed countries in the world out of the water (US is 23.8 percent, UK is 28.9 percent, Canada is 31.7 percent).[4] Or, the fascinating yet cautionary examples of existing matriarchies, like the Tibetan tribal community of the Mosuo, where sexual partners are taken solely at the leisure and direction of women either for pleasure or "sperm donation."[5] At first blush it sounds liberating, but at a deeper level, is it any better than the sexual dominance of patriarchy?

---

3   Alison Millington and Erin McDowell, "The 21 best countries in the world to live in if you're a woman," *Business Insider*, August 23, 2019.

4   GIWPS, "Women, Peace, and Security Index," accessed January 31, 2020.

5   Laura T. Garrison, "6 Modern Societies Where Women Rule," *Mental Floss*, March 3, 2017.

Those are just some of the facts sprinkled along this learning journey. Collecting and compiling stories and facts through a gender lens made it clear to see gender inequality is not just unfortunate, it's charting a pathway to ruin. Birthrates have fallen so low nearly half of the countries in the world aren't producing enough children to sustain their populations; the last time the earth was this warm was 125,000 years ago (and that didn't end well); globally, someone dies by suicide roughly every forty seconds (with men dying by suicide at twice the rate of women); and there are still forty million slaves in the world today, of whom 71 percent are women.[6]

Are all of these the fault of patriarchy? Maybe not, but as we uncover the roots of gender bias in the challenges of the world, it's clear we must be in an absolute race to replace the patriarchy. It's an ancient power-based system that is failing all of us, and it's time to envision something new if we are to save ourselves.

Gloria Steinem might call this book my "feminist awakening." And, maybe it is. But my awakening got so woke that I came to see you don't have to call yourself a feminist to believe in gender equality. Put simply, if you don't believe everyone, regardless of gender, should be treated equally, you're sexist. If you believe in doing everything possible to enable gender equality, congrats, you're an anti-sexist. Welcome to the club.

Vernacular aside, this journey is also an opportunity to build a deep appreciation for the fierce feminists, or

---

6   Linda Scott, *The Double X Economy: The Epic Potential of Women's Empowerment* (New York City: Farrar, Straus, and Giroux, 2020.), 145; Doyle Rice, "The last time the Earth was this warm was 125,000 years ago," *USA Today*, January 18, 2017; Hannah Ritchie, et al., "Suicide," Our World in Data, 2015; Scott, *The Double X,* 111.

anti-sexists, who have come before us. People like Kate Sheppard, the leader of New Zealand's feminist movement, whose work resulted in NZ becoming the first country where women earned the right to vote in 1893— and, more than two hundred years later, is already on its third female prime minister.[7] Or Flora Tristan, a French theorist, who in 1843 published an essay that argued the liberation of working classes couldn't be achieved without the corresponding emancipation of women.[8] Or the black activists Nellie May Quander, Ida B. Wells, and Mary Church Terrell, whose persistence in advocating that black women should be allowed to march alongside white women in the 1913 suffragists parade made them pioneers in demanding equal rights for women meant for *all* women.[9] There are *so many* anti-sexists that the history books have robbed us of the opportunity to really get to know and appreciate how we have benefited from their work.

While learning about these and other gender-rights pioneers, I found myself equally fascinated, appreciative, profoundly sad, and remorseful. Sad that it took me this far into my life to learn about them, and remorseful for the time I've wasted hustling through life without creating space to protect and advance the decades of progress these women worked to bequeath to my generation. Sad because it seems so many who devoted their lives, voices,

---

7   Kate Sheppard, "Encyclopedia Britannica," July 9, 2020.

8   Kristen R. Ghodsee, *Why Women Have Better Sex Under Socialism: And Other Arguments for Economic Independence* (New York: Bold Type Books, 2020.), 76.

9   Susan C. Bartoletti, *How Women Won the Vote: Alice Paul, Lucy Burns, and Their Big Idea* (New York: HarperCollins, 2020.), 34.

and work fighting for gender equality would never live to see their mission fully achieved—never getting to check "equality for women" off the old to-do list.

So, fellow anti-sexists, what if we put it on *our* to-do lists? Could the dreams of so many gender equality activists before us be realized within our lifetimes? And what if the check boxes on our list focus on what we need to build and create instead of smash and destroy? What if instead of *smashing the patriarchy*, we worked to *make the matriarchy*? What could that look like? What would it replace and protect? Might reframing a feminist rallying cry make the fight for equality more approachable for all?

I believe the universe puts us in the right place at the right time and being on this journey in 2020 was kismet. As I wiled my quarantined weekends away writing, the world around me was imploding at the hands of the coronavirus pandemic, an event that would force a global reckoning with leadership, equity, humanity, and social duty. In my home country, the United States, the reckoning hit particularly hard, exposing shortcomings in leadership; a willful under-investment in preparedness; glaring systemic inequities; and massive erosions in our shared sense of social duty. It tore open festering wounds in the collective skin of our society. As painful as it was to watch those wounds become exposed, it deepened my curiosity about what it will take to build something new on the other side. It also allowed me to spend much-needed time anchored to hope.

An early reader of my manuscript told me the pages that follow read more like a series of essays than a fully baked book, and maybe that's true. To me, it feels more like a journey journal; a product of my DIY distance-learning assignment to explore all there is to know about gender equality that resulted in a collection of opportunities to change how we think and behave, and, in doing so, create an entirely new world.

Whether essays, journal, or otherwise, the work you hold in your hands has changed my life. There is so much to gain from exploring what is working in the world—and not just for women, but for everyone. Over and over, sources and data prove when you improve life for women, life gets better for everyone. It is, frankly, exciting.

I resonate deeply with the puzzle analogy used throughout this book, because it invokes memories of my grandfather who loved puzzles. He'd frequently set up the card table in the parlor, dump out a million-piece puzzle, and chip away at it for days. He took pure pleasure in searching, finding, creating, and sharing his finished project. I see *How to Make the Matriarchy* much like one of his giant puzzles: there are a million pieces scattered across the globe needing to be uncovered, explored, and connected. I'm on a mission to find, understand, and connect the pieces that make up a masterpiece.

At its simplest, this book is rooted in my hope that once I understand the puzzle, I'll see more clearly my role in creating a more equitable world for our sons and daughters to inherit. At its grandest, by sharing my journey with you, I hope you will find your place too.

Because, as Marian Wright Edelmen and so many others like her have demonstrated in a lifetime of achieving what probably seemed impossible, one step at a time (or perhaps one "piece" at a time) is what it takes.

PART ONE

CHARTING THE JOURNEY

CHAPTER 1:

Let's Limber Up
with Lingo

If we're going to talk about patriarchies and matriarchies, equality and inequality, equity and inequity, we need to be on the same page with the lingo. So, I begin how I presume most books, research papers, dinner discussions, or kids' homework assignments begin these days. I did some googling.

According to *Merriam-Webster*:

Matriarchy[10]
1. a family, group, or state governed by a matriarch (a woman who rules or dominates a family, group, or state).
2. a system of social organization in which descent and inheritance are traced through the female line.

Patriarchy[11]
1. social organization marked by the supremacy of the father in the clan or family, the legal dependence of

---

10 *Merriam-Webster*, s.v. "Matriarchy," accessed July 18, 2020.
11 *Merriam-Webster*, s.v. "Patriarchy," accessed July 18, 2020.

wives and children, and the reckoning of descent and inheritance in the male line.

broadly: control by men of a disproportionately large share of power.

2. a society or institution organized according to the principles or practices of patriarchy.

Equality[12]

1. the quality or state of being equal.

Inequality [13]

1. the quality of being unequal or uneven, such as

   a. social disparity;
   b. disparity of distribution or opportunity;
   c. lack of evenness;
   d. the condition of being variable.

Equity[14]

1. a. justice according to natural law or right.

specifically: freedom from bias or favoritism.

   b. something that is equitable.

Inequity[15]

1. injustice, unfairness.
2. an instance of injustice or unfairness.

For those of you questioning the caliber of an author who starts by copying and pasting from the dictionary, stick with me. It became evident throughout my journey one of the challenges in organizing people around rallying

---

12 *Merriam-Webster*, s.v. "Equality," accessed July 18, 2020.

13 *Merriam-Webster*, s.v. "Inequality," accessed July 18, 2020.

14 *Merriam-Webster*, s.v. "Equity," accessed October 24, 2020.

15 *Merriam-Webster*, s.v. "Inequity," accessed October 24, 2020.

cries like "smash the patriarchy" or "achieve equality" is they don't mean the same thing to everyone. If I'm going to suggest we make the matriarchy, I need to be explicitly clear about what that means.

When I reached out to speak with Carla Golden, a professor in the Women's and Gender Studies department at my undergrad, Ithaca College, she underpinned the importance of level-setting on vernacular. Carla took a break from packing up her office to talk to me. Just a few days shy of retirement, her office clean-out had her looking back on over thirty years of teaching gender studies while both witnessing waves of feminism as they happened and later teaching about them in a historical context.

As we talked, Golden shared that previous feminist movements have generally been aligned on patriarchy as an overarching system that oppresses women. Whereas today, she finds her students use the word, say the word, but don't fully understand the reach of its structural nature. And, as Golden said, "you can't begin to change things until you really understand what you're up against."

I had a real revelation talking with Carla because I could see I shared a similar mindset to her students, and perhaps that's why "smash the patriarchy" wasn't working for me. I generally knew the phrase and the movement encompassed unlocking equal pay, eliminating violence against women, reducing maternal mortality rates, and promoting pro-women policies. But I didn't fully appreciate that solving any one of those things still wouldn't eliminate the deep structures rooted in supremacy, dependence, and a disproportionate amount of control by men, as *Merriam-Webster* so generously defines.

It's in the definitions of matriarchy and patriarchy themselves we see clues of the depth of the patriarchy's hold on us. The above definition of patriarchy is pretty darn specific. It's about power and domination along gender lines. Matriarchy? Well, it's a group governed by women. Upon comparing and contrasting these definitions, I pictured Mr. Merriam and Mr. Webster writing the incredibly simple definition of matriarchy, adjusting their spectacles, nodding, and saying, "Yes, yes, that should do. Moving on..."

Dictionary definitions aside, I also learned there is a distinction between a matriarchy and a matrilineal society. In a matriarchy, power and leadership lie with women through their social constructs. A matrilineal society, on the other hand, is one where inheritance passes through female lineage. It's an important distinction because matrilineal societies are often still controlled by male leaders, and while the passage of property follows matrilineal lines, it still often benefits men (i.e., property passes from a mother's brother to nephew, but never to the woman herself). Matrilineal societies are more common than true matriarchies, and while they may sound like progress, they can be quite oppressive. (By example, Burkina Faso, an African country that is easily one of the most oppressive and dangerous for women, is a matrilineal society.)[16]

Examining the definitions of equality and inequality was thought provoking as well. Equality (a state of being

---

16   Liza Debevec, "Setting the record straight: Matrilineal does not equal matriarchal," *Thrive*, January 2019.

equal) is simple and perhaps meaningless enough, but when contrasted against the definition of inequality (disparity of opportunity), that is when it starts to sink in that fighting for equality is one thing, but eliminating inequality may be entirely another.

The distinction between equity and equality is important as well. Something can be equal—for example, men and women having equal access to education. But differences along gender lines in the quality and content of the educational experience result in inequities in the outcomes achieved from that education.

Spending time unpacking words and how they are perceived was a gateway to the next inquiry. Patriarchy is all I've ever lived in, so the prevalence of male privilege was relatively easy to understand. I needed to know more about matriarchies if that was to be my rallying cry.

So what, I wondered, it is like to live in a matriarchy? Do any still exist? What can we learn about structure in societies that are governed by women? And I'm not talking about patriarchal societies with female leaders, but true, matriarchal societies where women govern and the structures around them support it. In short, women making it a woman's world, not a man's world.

CHAPTER 2:

Matriarchies: Where They Exist and What We Can Learn

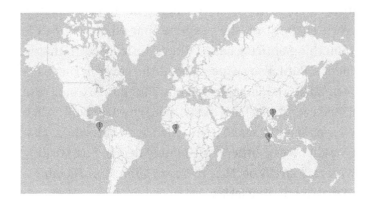

Four of the world's existing matriarchal cultures

"If you're going to use the word matriarchy, you had better really know what it means," warned Erin Keeley during our planned thirty-minute call that had stretched to ninety minutes. We were introduced by a mutual friend who knew Erin had studied Dravidian matriarchies with a religious scholar. Words matter, we agreed, and Erin wasn't the first person to question whether calling for a matriarchy was strong enough, or correct enough, or accurately matched my intent.

On the surface, if you break matriarchy down into its root words, *matri-* and *-archy,* the literal definition would be "mothers rule," which we freaking do, so the literal translation isn't necessarily a problem. But if we've learned anything about words, their literal definition can differ from perceived meaning. Matriarchal cultures and societies have existed throughout history, including present day, and they operate in many different ways. The word itself, then, can take on many interpretations.

Erin and I left our delightfully enlightening call a bit undecided. Erin was encouraging me to create a new word entirely, on the premise that what we need is something entirely new. I didn't disagree with that in theory. But I also suspect that if the cover of this book read "Make the Shibamergamerarchy," no one would read it, and everything I had to say about how we could do better would never make it into the hands of readers. That wouldn't work either. I ultimately decided on sticking with matriarchy because there are glimmers of goodness in matriarchal societies.

The most significant takeaway from exploring the word matriarchy is that matriarchal societies of the past and present are evidence things can be different. Erin shared that scholars believe the Dravidian matriarchy was incredibly egalitarian. That yes, there was role differentiation along gender lines, but the work was equal and the society was peaceful and inclusive. So inclusive that it was ultimately their demise when they openly welcomed invaders who would rape, kill, and send the remaining Dravidians (and their matriarchal ways) into hiding.

"The main principle of these traditions is that feminine energy is generative," Erin said. For the Dravidians, they called upon the collaborative and peaceful leadership styles of their female leaders because "when you're cultivating the same rice fields for thirty-five thousand years, you can't escape. You have to figure out how to get along."

Learning about the Dravidians from Erin was a tremendous lesson in history, but it was (really) ancient history. It caused me to wonder, are there modern-day matriarchies we can learn from, good, bad, or otherwise? Turns out, there are.

1
MOSUO

Located near the border of Tibet and the Yunnan and Sichuan provinces, Mosuo is an ancient tribal community of about forty thousand people. In their social structure, women are considered the leaders socially, economically, and sexually.[17]

I have to admit, reading about the sexual liberation of Mosuo women was so different from my lived experience. I was both intrigued and curious about what living this lifestyle might be like.

In Mosuo, marriage as a long-standing union between a man and a woman simply doesn't exist. Instead, men and

17   Garrison, "6 Modern Societies."

women practice what is a known as "walking marriage," which writer Hannah Booth coins as "an elegant term for what are essentially furtive, nocturnal hook-ups." Lovers, called "axia," are taken completely at the leisure and direction of women. Booth goes on to explain that "a man's hat hung on the door handle of a woman's quarters is a sign to other men not to enter. These range from one-night stands to regular encounters that deepen into exclusive, life-long partnerships—and may or may not end in pregnancy. But couples never live together, and no one says, 'I do.'"[18] Quite simply, the role of axia are for women's pleasure and procreation.

Here's where I paused to think about how freeing it would be to have that kind of control and access to pleasure without societal backlash. Having grown up in a traditional and conservative setting, I was taught to view sex as something to reserve and control to preserve my reputation. This alternative, pleasure-based construct with women at the helm was both fascinating and exhilarating.

Mosuo women may have as many axia as they like. Should a hat-handled night result in pregnancy, Mosuo women rarely know who the father is, mostly because the social construct of fatherhood doesn't exist. The concept of a nuclear family exists in an entirely different form.

The Mosuo live in large households with extended family, with the eldest female as the head of the household. Lineage is traced through the female side of the family, and property is passed down along those lines. Children are raised in their mother's household and take

---

18   Hannah Booth, "The kingdom of women: The society where a man is never the boss," *The Guardian*, April 1, 2017.

her name. Men remain in their mother's household for the duration of their life and contribute as sons and uncles instead of spouses.

Booth reports that "although men have no paternal responsibilities... they have considerable responsibility as uncles to their sisters' children. In fact, along with elderly maternal great-uncles, who are often the households' second-in-charge, younger uncles are the pivotal male influence on children."[19]

While this all sounds liberating compared to the patriarchal structures, the more I thought critically about Mosuo, I realized it still bears similarities to the most extreme forms of patriarchy. I started to wonder where consent plays into all of this, how the men feel in this society, and if this matriarchy is really something to admire. Consider that if you scratch the surface you see that in this construct, women's power still depends on procreation. To create the opportunity to *be* a matriarch, one must birth her followers. This means that for most young women in Mosuo, their main objective is still *to have sex and make babies.* Not exactly progressive in that light.

As in many extreme patriarchies where birthing boys is revered, in Mosuo, birthing girls is revered. Without female heirs, there is no future for your lineage. In my research, there were even examples of women with no female heirs arranging "adoptions" for baby girls. The more I considered this, the less I considered Mosuo's matriarchy progressive.

In 2006, Choo WaiHong ditched her career as a corporate lawyer in Singapore to travel, specifically to China to

_____
19   Ibid.

explore her ancestry. She spent time in Mosuo embedding in their society, which she documents in her book, *The Kingdom of Women.* What she ultimately discovers is that Mosuo society is indeed changing, as younger women don't want to live for motherhood. WaiHong writes that elder generations still practice walking marriage, as do many women in their forties. However, "about half of women in their thirties live with their 'partners'—the fathers of their young children."[20]

It remains to be seen how the Mosuo culture will evolve as the younger generations age and if their version of matriarchy will survive.

2
AKAN

The Akan are a cultural group residing throughout Ghana, most predominant in the southern regions, and are represented in various sub-groups, each with their own names. Ancient Akan society, which can be traced back to Paleolithic times, was established as a matriarchy, with the "queen mother" serving as the ruler of the clan. Queen mothers ruled over all aspects of the clan, setting values, policies, practices, and traditions. The role of queen mother was passed through matrilineal blood lines, and new states could only be established by queen mothers.

The Akan matriarchy has struggled to survive and was particularly in danger during the colonialization of Africa, in which Western worldviews threatened to swallow up matriarchical leadership in favor of kingship

---

20 Ibid.

and European worldviews about male dominance. Researcher Eva Meyerowitz studied Africa in the 1940s and observed the threat in action, including power transfers from queen mothers to kings, updating cultural lore to change female deities into male deities, and, culturally, men becoming ashamed to have allowed themselves to be ruled or dominated by women for so long. Colonialists bypassed women leaders, negotiating only with male chiefs, so their influence dwindled.

Things didn't look good when Ghana achieved independence in 1957 and the new government didn't restore queen mothers to leadership roles. While queen motherhood wasn't completely erased from history, their role became mostly ceremonial. Today, male chiefs do retain a tremendous amount of social, political, and economic clout, and with 80 percent of Ghana's land under their control, it's questionable whether a matriarchy does indeed exist.[21]

So why am I still writing about the Akan?

Most clans, neighborhoods, and villages do still (or once again) have a queen mother. This tradition is more common in the southern regions but gaining popularity in the north, where these female cultural leaders are called Pognaa.

There is a serious women's movement to restore the voice of these female leaders in society. In her article, "Meet the Queen Mothers: 10,000 Amazing Women Taking Back Power in Africa," journalist Veronique Mistiaen paints the picture of resurgence through the lens of a 2015 swearing-in ceremony of the newly elected members

21 Garrison, "6 Modern Societies."

of the National Council of Women Traditional Leaders. Describing the scene, she writes,

> Greeting each other warmly, they take their seats under the canopy across from the dignitaries on a dais in a courtyard in Legon, a suburb of Accra, talking on their smartphones and consulting their tablets, majestic in their kentes—the distinctive hand-woven cloth in the bright colours and bold patterns of their respective communities. These formidable women are the twenty-first century incarnation of the traditional Queen Mothers of Ghana and they are ready to reclaim their power. The assembled ministers, chiefs, academics and journalists cannot help but stare in awe as one Queen Mother approaches the microphone and issues a pithy warning, "These beautiful clothes that you admire so much are full of knowledge. Don't underestimate us."[22]

The work of these women throughout Ghana to regain power and bring attention to women's issues is inspiring and felt similar to women's movements happening in other parts of the world. What I think is a key differentiation, however, is they are working to *rebuild* a modernized version of a leadership structure that was once alive and well before it was stolen from them. It's not about power or winning. Their ultimate goal is not to be restored as true matriarchs, but rather to build a new version that improves the evolution of their society and, at a minimum, restores their voice at policy-making tables. A key initiative is to establish full representation

---

22 Veronique Mistiaen, "Meet the queen mothers: 10,000 amazing women taking back power in Africa," *The Telegraph*, December 3, 2014.

and voting rights in the regional and national Houses of Chiefs (they can currently attend but have no voting rights).

At first, it was sad to read about the loss of what seemed to be a perfectly fine society where women were valued for cultural, spiritual, and practical reasons. That sadness turned to rage when I considered this loss happened thanks to the influence of European and Western values (a.k.a. patriarchy).

But instead of settling on rage, what I learned about the Akan (and matriarchies in Ghana in general) is a valuable lesson in the resilience of women and their willpower to organize and recreate. The evolution of the Akan's matriarchy is a valuable tale in the (re) making of a matriarchy.

3
BRIBRI

Living on a reserve in the Limon province of Costa Rica, the Bribri are an indigenous group of just over thirteen thousand members. Their matriarchy is organized into clans made up of extended family with the mother or females in leadership roles. Tribal lineage passes through the mother, and grandmothers are revered and respected as the keepers of knowledge and culture. In terms of progressive, inclusive societies, the Bribri provide some interesting insights.

The Bribri culture is rooted in honoring and replicating the symbiosis created by mother nature. Much like mother nature, women sit at the center of this culture as community-focused guides for the survival of all. Author Courtney Parker writes, "The new wave of feminism that is being led by las mujeres de América Latina (the women of Latin America) is community focused. It's not about proving what one woman can do on her own or proving that she can succeed as a man in a 'man's world'. It is by exceedingly stark contrast about proving what one can do for the greater community, and perhaps as the scope naturally broadens, what one can do for the world."[23]

Bribri strive to preserve tribal traditions, language, and culture as the outside world tries to invade and influence. Chiquita (the banana company) has a large presence in their region and brings with it their globalized ways of thinking: preference for male laborers, use of pesticides, and mass production, which are in direct contrast to the core values of the Bribri matriarchy and also introduce health risks for their people.[24]

In response to that challenge, Bribri women are crafting community-oriented responses, at the center of which is creating other opportunities for revenue for the community so as not to become reliant on Chiquita for survival. They are exploring ecotourism, organic agriculture, crafts, traditional food and beverage, and educational opportunities. Their commitment to producing "wealth in partnership with nature" is an interesting concept and is likely a piece of the puzzle when it comes to making the matriarchy.[25]

As if their theory on women in the world and commitment to preservation aren't enough to love, one of their sacred rituals involves a traditional cacao drink only

---

23   Ibid.

24   Admin, "Bribri: Matriarchy and Feminism Living in CR," *The Costarican Times*, February 20, 2014.

25   Ibid.

allowed to be prepared by women (cacao is thought to contain a spiritual superiority). A village in Costa Rica with women at the helm who want equality, what's best for their community, who believe chocolate is spiritually superior, and who live in a village that (I imagine) smells like chocolate all the time? Sign me up.

4
MINANGKABAU (NOT QUITE A MATRIARCHY, BUT A PROGRESSIVE MATRILINEAL SOCIETY)

Home to four million residents, the Minangkabau of West Sumatra, Indonesia, make up the largest known matrilineal society in the world and "devote everything to women." [26] An interesting juxtaposition, the Minangkabau people are devout Muslims, a faith that goes to great lengths to honor men over women. However, the Minangkabau people interpret the teachings of the Koran in ways that allow for a unique balance of power and have even created their own loopholes to concurrently honor Muslim requirements and their matrilineal society.

In Minangkabau society, women rule the domestic realm while men inhabit the political and spiritual roles. For example, the role of chief of each clan is always a male, but is selected (and removed when necessary) solely by women. The Minangkabau's participate in traditional marriage between women and men. Upon marriage, the man moves into the woman's home, where the woman maintains her own sleeping quarters. And, while the man may sleep with her, he must depart each morning to eat breakfast at his mother's home. [27]

---

26   Danielle Shapiro, "Indonesia's Minangkabau: The World's Largest Matrilineal Society," *The Daily Beast*, July 13, 2017.

27   Ibid.

In researching the Minangkabau, a theme which came up over and over again was the sense that power and authority are shared. Nearly all decisions, whether in the home or in the management of the clan, require consensus between men and women. Something I found inspiring in general, but especially inspiring considering their Islamic faith and its specific rules about the roles of the sexes.

For example, Islamic law dictates, in part, that sons must inherit twice as much as daughters. This would appear to be in direct conflict with the Minangkabau tradition of Adat, which dictates inheritance must pass through matrilineal lines. How do they make it work? They have established "high inheritance," which is property that includes home and land; and "low inheritance," which is what a father can pass out of his professional earnings. The Minangkabau practice both concurrently and, quite cleverly, point out that Islamic law doesn't *prohibit* women from inheriting.

In reading interviews with Minangkabau members, many of the women were highly educated (doctors, university professors, and the like), as were the men, and both men and women seemed content with their roles and sense of equality. Overall, I was impressed with how the Minangkabau have built and sustained their society both equally and with a clear deference to the importance of women. It seems an attractive example of a matriarchy, and even more so when you pause to consider that the Minangkabau make up about 3 percent of Indonesia's total population. (In the US, it would be akin to the entire state of Pennsylvania living in honor of women.) Perhaps proof that when it comes to making the matriarchy, it can start with a part of the whole changing their ways.

5
THE ANIMAL KINGDOM

When I set out to write this book, I certainly didn't think I'd spend any time talking about animals other than humans. But as this fascinating journey unfolded, a few animal matriarchies wove their way into stories, adding color, knowledge, and a sense of place to this exploration.

Existing research has found there are only eight mammal species that exemplify female leadership: hyenas, killer whales, lions, spotted hyenas, bonobos, lemurs, and elephants.

Most interesting of these is the bonobo. Bonobos and chimpanzees are human's closest genetic relatives: 99 percent of our DNA is the same. Chimpanzees live as a patriarchy and bonobos a matriarchy. In chimpanzee society the lowest-status male still ranks higher than the highest-status female, but in bonobo society the sisterhood prevails and the females run the show.

What can we learn from observing the patriarchy versus the matriarchy of our genetic neighbors? In groups of chimps extreme violence reigns supreme. Male chimps guard their female mates, and female chimps have no say in their sexual partners. Groups of male chimps have been known to occasionally kill other groups to gain control of territory. Infanticide is common.

The bonobos, on the other hand, are peaceful, egalitarian, and "famed for their use of sex to solve every problem, in any situation and, crucially, with any gender."[28] Older

---

28 Harriet Marsden, "International Women's Day: What are matriarchies, and where are they now?" *Independent,* March 8, 2018.

females serve as troop leaders. Bonobos almost never kill each other and share food and resources with the group in more egalitarian ways. Female bonding and cooperation are common, even as bonobos move between bonobo groups that aren't related.

Aggression certainly happens, and female bonobos are physically smaller than their male counterparts and often lose one-on-one scuffles with males. However, Takeshi Furuichi, who studies bonobos in the Democratic Republic of Congo, has observed that the secret to their success is working together. Furuishci says, "When more than two females collaborate to fight males, 100 percent of the time, females win."[29]

THE TAKEAWAYS

I had a lot of feelings after completing this initial research. I read theories that much of the world had once been a matriarchy only to be lost through colonialism, industrialization, and westernization. I had pangs of jealousy toward the matriarchies that seemed sexually liberated, though I wondered how the men in these villages really feel about the construct. There were glimmers of men's movements toward greater equality in some places. It made me wonder if any leadership and power constructs organized around gender can ever be truly happy. It made me wonder if I still want to make the matriarchy.

But what I also learned is that real matriarchy is not about power. It's about equality. Heide Göttner-Abendroth, matriarchy expert and founder of the International

---

29 Lesley Evans Ogden, "What animals tell us about female leadership," *BBC*, September 26, 2018.

Academy Hagia for Modern Matriarchal Studies, explains the aim of matriarchy "is not to have power over others and over nature, but to follow maternal values, i.e. to nurture the natural, social, and cultural life based on mutual respect."[30] Where patriarchy relies on power over others, matriarchy is about mutual respect and power from within. Or, as I like to think from here on out, the patriarchy is about power over others, and matriarchy is about power of inclusion. That's the future I want to make.

Exploring matriarchies was fascinating and fun, but none are exactly a blueprint for the kind of modern construct I seek to envision. The lessons I'll carry forward are the power of inclusion, recognizing there was life before patriarchy, ways to build back after patriarchy, and that male-dominance is learned and, with effort, can be un-learned too. With all that in mind, however, it's time to keep exploring for more clues.

30   Marsden, "International Women's Day."

CHAPTER 3:

Is the Matriarchy Already Here?

———

As with any journey, experiencing periods of self-doubt is to be expected. Still early in my research, I was wrestling with the trajectory of this book. Is "the matriarchy" something we really want to make? Is it already made? Is it happening as we speak and this will all be irrelevant by the time I actually publish this thing?

The first moment that gave me pause was a conversation with my mother. My mother was born in 1950, raised in a middle-class home in upstate New York, and was an elementary school teacher for thirty-five years before retiring. When I first told her I was writing this book, her first reaction was to ask, "Do you really think women still aren't equal?" When I replied with a resounding "yes!" we ended up in a discussion dissecting why she truly believed women now had all of the same opportunities and equalities as men. We ultimately agreed to disagree, which is not uncommon for us.

But then, it happened again. This time, I shared the idea of this book with a CFO of a large company who, I'd estimate, is in her fifties. Again, she paused and asked me if I really thought women didn't have equal opportunities. She went on to explain that, as a woman with a long career in the male-dominated field of finance, she never felt like she had been at a disadvantage. From her view, she had promotions, good compensation, and the flexibility she needed to raise her daughter. Interestingly enough, she said her college-aged daughter had often expressed her own frustrations with barriers to gender equality, but she struggled to see it from her point of view. She agreed my topic would be interesting to explore, but genuinely seemed to believe gender equality had been achieved long-ago.

To add fuel to my uncertainty, at the same time I was embarking on this journey, I accepted a position as the interim president and CEO of a mid-sized non-profit organization, whose staff of fifty-one employees was made up of forty-seven women and four men, with all of the leadership roles, including the board chair, held by women. News bits about gains being made in equality and women earning prestigious leadership roles started catching my eye.

Could I have all of this wrong? Is equality already here?

I will concede that your opinion on this (and perhaps all things in life) is rooted in perception. For the purposes of my mom's life, to a middle-class white woman who out-earned and out-saved my dad her entire life and is now blissfully enjoying her retirement, the world is equal. For the CFO, another successful white woman, her personal experience felt equal. And there are many other women, predominantly middle- and upper-class white women, whose experiences leave them believing gender equality is a thing of the past, especially when they compare their lives to those of their own mothers.

I will admit, previous to this journey my life felt relatively equal, though I always suspected something not quite right lurking below the surface. Having spent my entire professional life in non-profits, which are predominantly staffed by women, I was even fooled into wondering if my profession had cracked some secret code.

But mine and my mother's experience are not the norm. As educated middle-class white women, we enjoyed many privileges that put us within reach of equality. And going about life living predominantly through the lens of personal experience creates exactly the kind of complicity needed to prevent progress. When I looked beyond my own stories and social circles, evidence was everywhere that gender inequality still runs rampant— especially when you begin to layer in race, sexual identity, geography, and more.

Super Tuesday 2020 helped snap me back into reality. At one point, the field of candidates vying to be the democratic party nominee included six women: one African American, one Samoan-American, and four Caucasian women. Among the male candidates, the pool included two African Americans, one Latin American, one Asian American, and eleven white men. A total of twenty-one candidates in all, with nearly half the field being non-male and non-white.

Alas, Super Tuesday came and went, and while one female was still technically in the running, she had just one delegate from American Samoa and no viable path to the nomination. We were left with two white males, Joe Biden and Bernie Sanders, as our choices.

Elizabeth Warren, once a front-runner, dropped out of the race on March 5, 2020. In remarks following her departure, she was asked what her message would be to women and girls who were left with two white men to decide between. Getting emotional, she responded, "One of the hardest parts of this is... all those little girls who are going to have to wait four more years. That's going to be hard."[31] To further cement my resolve, the UN study cited at the beginning of this book was released on the same day. To refresh, that study found "91 percent of men and 86 percent of women hold at least one bias against women in relation to politics, economics, education, violence or reproductive rights." The same study found that "almost half of people feel men are superior political leaders, more than 40 percent believe men make better business leaders, and nearly a third of both men and women believe it's acceptable for a man to beat his wife."[32]

Further, in 2015, 193 countries agreed on the UN Sustainable Development Goals (SDGs): a blueprint to fix global problems like climate change, hunger and poverty, work and economic growth, and achieve gender equality and reduce inequalities by 2030. In June of 2019, the Equal Measures 2030 partnership published a gender index which found that "no country was on track to achieve gender equality by 2030."[33] In fact, at the current pace,

31 Libby Cathey, "Little girls will have to wait 4 more years, Warren says, as 2020 race loses viable female candidates," *ABC News*, March 8, 2020.

32 Ford, "Nine out of 10."

33 Equal Measures 2030, *2019 Em2030 SDG Gender Index*, 2019.

sixty-seven of the 193 countries in the agreement will not achieve *any* of the key gender equality targets by 2030.[34] Glaring evidence of inequality was creeping into the lens of my own life as well. My new role was for an organization serving survivors of domestic and sexual violence. During my employee on-boarding, I learned some shocking statistics, including: one in seven women and one in eighteen men have been stalked; one in five women and one in fifty-nine men in the US is raped during his or her lifetime; one in three female murder victims and one in twenty male murder victims are killed by intimate partners; and finally, 94 percent of all murder-suicide victims are female.[35]

So, no, dear readers and friends, gender equality has very much *not* been achieved.

Are women's lives today better than the lives of Elizabeth Cady Stanton and Susan B. Anthony, who were fighting for suffrage at a time when women couldn't inherit property or custody of their children or hold a job and legally keep their own wages? Are our lives better than those of women during WWII, who were invited into the working world like never before only to be sent back home to keep the household once the war was over? Is my life better than that of my mother and grandmothers?

The answer, for me, is undoubtedly yes, for which I am profoundly grateful. However, the answer, for many women around the world and in my own country and local community, is no.

---

34 Liz Ford, "Not one single country set to achieve gender equality by 2030," *The Guardian*, June 3, 2019.

35 Domestic Violence, *National Coalition Against Domestic Violence*, n.d.

Gloria Steinem's book *Outrageous Acts and Everyday Rebellions* was first published in 1983, then updated in 1995 and again in 2018. It includes articles, essays, and interviews from as early as the 1970s. The book is cleverly designed so you don't know the date of the writing until you reach the end of each story. In reading this book, I was startled by how many stories I was certain would end with a more recent date, only to find tales of inequality from the 1970s and 1980s that could easily be headlines today. Steinem herself, in an updated preface written in 2018, says, "Altogether, when I see these essays being handed down to another generation of readers, I don't know whether to celebrate or mourn. I would feel rewarded if all were so out of date that they ranked right up there with 'Why Roosevelt Can't Win a Second Term.'"[36]

In 1980 she wrote that "feminist writers and theorists tend to avoid the future by lavishing all our analytical abilities on what's wrong with the present," and "we need pragmatic planners and visionary futurists, but can we think of even one feminist five-year plan?"[37]

I believe there are versions of plans out there, and I intend to use the future chapters to serve as a "visionary futurist" and boldly envision what equality might look like in the areas where we most need empowering and use modern day examples of evidence to get there.

So, here we go.

---

36 Gloria Steinem, *Outrageous Acts and Everyday Rebellions* (London: Picador, 2019), xix.

37 Ibid, 197.

CHAPTER 4:

Current Status of Women in the World

Researching far flung matriarchies around the world was fun and enlightening, but they are only a small piece of the puzzle and not necessarily relatable when envisioning progress for developed countries. I wondered, Who else in the world can we learn from? It turns out there is a new-found wealth of data to track the quality of life for women in countries around the world.

THE BEST PLACES IN THE WORLD TO BE A WOMAN

The 2019 Women, Peace, and Security Index (GIWPS) "is a comprehensive measure of women's wellbeing spanning three dimensions: inclusion (economic, social, political); justice (formal laws and informal discrimination); and security (at the family, community, and societal levels)." Published by the Georgetown Institute for Women, Peace, and Security, the 2019 report is an update to the inaugural report published in 2017.[38]

---

38   GIWPS, "The Dimensions," accessed September 22, 2020.

I read the ninety-two-page report from cover to cover. Doing so put a lot in perspective.

The report ranks 167 countries who represent more than 98 percent of the world's population. Within the previously mentioned dimensions (inclusion, justice, and security) each country is measured and ranked on eleven key indicators: *inclusion* measures education, financial inclusion, employment, cellphone use, and parliamentary representation; *justice* measures legal discrimination, son bias, and discriminatory norms; and *security* measures intimate partner violence, community safety, and organized violence.[39]

So, what does the world look like for women through these eleven lenses?

The Best Places to Be a Woman:[40]

1. Norway

2. Switzerland

3. Denmark (tie)

3. Finland (tie)

5. Iceland

6. Austria

7. United Kingdom

8. Luxembourg

9. Netherlands (tie)

9. Sweden (tie)

---

39   Ibid.

40   GIWPS, "Women, Peace, and Security Index," accessed September 22, 2020.

The Worst Places to Be a Woman:

167. Yemen

166. Afghanistan

165. Syria

164. Pakistan

163. South Sudan

162. Iraq

161. DR Congo

160. Central African Republic

159. Mali

158. Libya

Still Better than the United States:

11. Canada

12. Estonia

13. Slovenia

14. New Zealand

15. Spain

16. Ireland

17. Germany (tie)

17. Portugal (tie)

19. USA

I will admit, when I first read this I was mostly focused on why the US barely breaks the top twenty and how frustrated I was that this "superpower" I call home is far from the best place to be a woman. Further, it was not lost on me that if I were to return to the country where some of my ancestors immigrated from (Ireland) I'd be in better shape than I am in the country they expected to promise a better life for future generations.

Stepping out from behind my own lenses, however, I began to appreciate that achieving equality is going to be very relative depending on where in the world you are a woman. For instance, while I'm frustrated the 2020 US Congress is only 23.7 percent female, in Papa New Guinea women have no seats in the national legislature, and in eighteen other countries the number of women in parliament is in the single digits.[41] While I lament my lack of paid maternity leave, in China "son bias" can drive mothers to find out the gender of the baby in utero so as to consider aborting if it's a girl. Cell phone use, something so seemingly ubiquitous and basic, is a lifeline to safety, banking, and education that women are denied in other parts of the world.

If we are in a race to replace the patriarchy, it's important we appreciate that around the world, women are assigned very different starting lines.

Alas, my goal here is to explore as a visionary futurist where we need to go. That's not to say I don't care about those further behind in the race. Rather, it's those of us privileged with a better starting position who have an obligation to understand how we got there and design strategies to ensure we don't leave those further back behind completely.

---

41 "Women, Peace, and Security Index," 13.

WHO ARE THE STANDOUTS, AND HOW DID THEY GET THERE?

The standout is Iceland. They were ranked number one in the 2017 report, and in 2019 they are the only country who scores in the top third across the board in each of the eleven indicators.[42] Substantiating this finding, Iceland has been found by the World Economic Forum to be the most gender-equal country in the world eleven times in a row.[43] In the GIWPS, even though their combined final score placed them at number five in the 2019 rankings, this is only because their Nordic neighbors made *tiny* increases in point values to "overtake" them. And it's clear the Nordics may be on to something in general:

2019 Women Peace and Security Index Top Ranked Countries Compared to Their 2017 Ranking

Country	2019 Ranking	2017 Ranking
Norway	1	2
Switzerland	2	3
Denmark	3	12
Finland	3	6
Iceland	5	1

Nordics have achieved a lot in gender equality and are basically holding their ground. We'll explore the elements that make their societies so favorable throughout this book and in depth in Chapter 13. Ultimately, we'll find the fact Nordics lead on peace, equality, and happiness indices

42 Ibid, 11.

43 "Why gender parity matters," *World Economic Forum*, December 19, 2019.

is a product of decades of policy and culture-shaping work with exactly those outcomes in mind.

Equality and happiness in the Nordic region were somethings I had seen before, so it was the other somewhat surprising stories on progress in this data that captured my attention.

RWANDA

Rwanda has the highest global parliamentary representation by women at 61.3 percent. Yes. Rwanda. Their overall position in the index rose twenty-nine places from ninety-nine in 2017 to sixty-five in 2019. Contributing factors to their rise were women's financial inclusion rising from 30 percent to 45 percent and women's sense of community safety going from 82.1 percent to 85.1 percent.[44] Compared broadly across the ratings, Rwanda has some of the highest rankings for women's employment and sense of community safety, but also some of the lowest scores for number of years of schooling and cell phone use among women.

Providing even further context, the 2020 Global Gender Gap Index produced by the World Economic Forum ranked Rwanda number nine overall (behind Iceland, Norway, Finland, Sweden, Nicaragua, New Zealand, Ireland, and Spain) and number four in the world for political empowerment. Overall, Rwanda has closed 79.1 percent of its gender gap.[45]

It's clear Rwanda is making great gains towards women's equality. So, how did they get there, and what can we learn?

---

44   "Women, Peace, and Security Index,"13.

45   "Why gender parity matters," *World Economic Forum*, Dec 19, 2019.

In April of 1994, extremists in Rwanda's majority Hutu population embarked on a deliberate genocide to eliminate the minority Tutsi population. It is estimated that in just a one-hundred-day span, between eight-hundred thousand and one million Rwandans were murdered and another two million or more fled the country.

Previous to the genocide, women were second-class citizens. It was practically unheard of for women to be in leadership roles, work outside the home, own land, or have any financial empowerment. When the violence came to an end, however, records estimated that Rwanda's remaining population of roughly six million was anywhere from 60-80 percent female.[46] In order for Rwanda to rebuild, it would have to do so with the predominantly female population that remained.

In her book, *Rwandan Women Rising*, author Swanee Hunt interviews more than seventy Rwandan women who took on critical roles rebuilding their communities and country. She writes, "Women moved from cleaning buildings to reconstructing them. They farmed and started businesses. Throughout the country, they created stability in the aftermath of unspeakable violence."[47]

Women in leadership roles brought first-hand experience of the challenges they had faced and materialized momentum for change quickly. Decades of oppression were undone in the span of a few years as legislation was passed allowing Rwandan women to inherit property, open bank accounts, obtain loans without their

46   Gregory Warner, "It's the No.1 Country for Women in Politics—But Not in Daily Life," *NPR*, July 29, 2016.

47   Shereen Hall, "How Women Rebuilt Rwanda," *Inclusive Security*, accessed October 29, 2020.

husband's permission, and access incentives designed to support young women attending college to study predominantly male-dominated subjects.

In 2003, Rwanda passed a new constitution that codified a quota reserving a minimum 30 percent of parliamentary seats for women. This move was seen as encouraging and reflecting upon the rise of women in both informal and formal leadership that had helped restore the country. At the same time, the government made a commitment to prioritize education for girls and the appointment of women to leadership roles.[48]

Rwanda's new president, Paul Kagame, was a deliberate partner in building a more gender-equal society. Journalist Gregory Warner writes, "Kagame vowed to not merely play catch-up to the West but leapfrog ahead of it."[49] Here, Rwanda provides another important lesson: gender equality can be achieved when prioritized by men in leadership, and it will need to be if we are to succeed. Kagame demonstrated any leader can set the stage for inclusion. Kagame struck the vision, but the country embraced it, going beyond the 30 percent minimum requirement, rising at one time to 64 percent and landing at the global high of 61.3 percent today.[50]

There is still resistance to change, of course. Justine Uvuza, the former head of the legal division of Rwanda's Ministry of Gender and Family Promotion, examined the public and private lives of Rwanda's female parliamentarians

---

48 Ibid.

49 Ibid.

50 Alex Thornton, "These countries have the most women in parliament," *World Economic Forum*, February 12, 2019.

in her doctoral dissertation. In Uvuza's interviews with female parliamentarians, they reported their husbands still expected them to "make sure his shoes are polished, his shirts are ironed, and his water is in the bathtub."[51] In response, leaders are launching programs to bring men and boys into the conversation, and Rwanda's Ministry of Gender and Family Promotion seeks to "prevent discrimination from being seeded, starting with instilling gender-equity principles in children."[52]

Emma Furaha Rubagumya, who fled Rwanda during the genocide but returned and now serves as a first-term parliamentarian, summed up Rwanda's journey best: "We have frameworks, we have policies, we have laws, we have enforcement mechanisms... We've walked a journey, we've registered good achievements, but we still need to go further to make sure that at some point we shall be totally free of all imbalances."[53]

By no means should we gloss over the atrocity of the Rwandan genocide, and the lesson here is certainly not that the model for achieving equality for women is a byproduct of war. Rather, I think the lesson is how quickly gender equality can begin to improve when women flood the most important societal structures.

SWITZERLAND

Ranked third overall in 2017 and rising to second in 2019 (the highest of any country outside of the Nordic regions), Switzerland piqued my curiosity and led me down a twisting tale of the history of women's equality there.

---

51 Rania Abouzeid, "Remaking Rwanda," *National Geographic,* November 2019, 92.

52 Ibid.

53 Ibid.

I was shocked to learn that in Switzerland women weren't granted the right to vote countrywide until 1971. Early in the twentieth century, as other countries around the world were giving women the right to vote, Swiss women had to campaign until 1959 for the opportunity to even appear on a national referendum (how all Swiss laws are enacted). In the national vote of 1959, women were still denied, with 67 percent of the country voting no.[54]

I had to let that sink in for a minute. In just one generation before my own, the majority of Swiss voters (remember: just men!) believed women shouldn't vote.

It wasn't until the option reached the national vote again in 1971 that popular opinion flipped, and women won the right to vote with 66 percent of Swiss voters (still just men!) in favor. Even then, however, this was only the right to vote in national elections. Local cantons (similar to US states or counties) could still decide local voting rights. The last canton to grant voting rights to women was Appenzell Innerrhoden in 1991, after the Swiss Supreme Court forced every canton to comply with a new Equal Rights Amendment on the books. The new amendment also ushered in changes like prohibiting public schools from demanding higher grades from girls than boys. It was only in 1992 that Swiss women no longer lost their citizenship if they married a foreigner. And it wasn't until 2013 that married women were permitted to keep their birth names.[55]

Again, I'm letting it sink in Switzerland, a highly developed country with one of the oldest democracies in the

54   Stefanie Kurt, "Nation of Brothers with Late Arriving Sisters," *NCCR,* May 12, 2016.

55   Ibid.

world (with voting dating back to 1291) had female residents without some very basic equal rights, including voting, during my lifetime. As journalist Robert Krulwich put it in his article titled "Non! Nein! No! A Country That Wouldn't Let Women Vote Till 1971," "Democracy and progress aren't always friends."[56]

I tried to reconcile how a country who lagged so far behind in equal rights for women well into my lifetime still outranks countries who have had it for much longer.

I suspect it has something to do with the fact that the Peace and Security Index measures just that—peace and security—in a place that has always been relatively peaceful and secure. Women are well educated; they have financial inclusion and cell phones; intimate partner violence is very low; and perception of community safety is very high.

While the Swiss have made rapid progress in recent years, all too familiar remnants of inequality remain: Swiss women earn about 20 percent less than men in the same positions and have the second highest rate of part-time employment among member countries in the Organisation for Economic Co-operation and Development (OECD).[57] These factors are attributed to females working part time jobs to allow time to carry the majority of family-raising duties.

Additionally, Switzerland may be the second most peaceful and secure place for women to live, but it is familiar

---

56 Robert Krulwich, "Non! Nein! No! A Country That Wouldn't Let Women Vote Till 1971," *National Geographic*, August 26, 2016.

57 Federal Statistical Office, "Wage gap," accessed September 22, 2020; OECD, "Part-time employment rate," accessed September 22, 2020.

gaps in paid parental leave and affordable childcare that fuel the country's continued women's movement. In June of 2019, thousands of women participated in a nation-wide strike to signal their frustration over gender inequalities in one of the richest countries in the world.[58] Hoping to influence change in the fall elections, women marched to call attention to women holding the bulk of responsibility for childcare and domestic work, to put more women in parliament, and to encourage gender diversity across their society and economy.

And their efforts worked. As a result of the October 2019 elections, the number of female parliamentarians rose to eighty-five, a 10 percent increase over the outgoing parliament.[59]

WHY THE STORIES OF RWANDA AND SWITZERLAND MATTER

These stories matter so much on this journey because they demonstrate how change and progress are possible within a generation. If we hit the gas pedal on prioritizing gender rights and equality and putting women in leadership, change can follow rather quickly.

When looking at the laundry list of inequalities patriarchy perpetuates and how long the systemic oppression has been able to hold on, it can feel downright impossible to expect improvements in one lifetime. But Rwanda and Switzerland show us there is possibility, in both developed and developing countries. And that's just the kind of hope we need to inspire us to pursue change.

58   Anna Schaverien and Nick-Cumming Bruce, "Swiss Women Strike Nationwide to Protest Inequalities," *The New York Times*, June 14, 2019.

59   Ibid.

CHAPTER 5: GOAL-SETTING:

Where to Begin?

———

Advancing gender equality is certainly not a new topic, but we may have better data than ever before. Much of the data I was viewing, like the 2017 and 2019 Women, Peace, and Security Indexes; the inaugural Gender Social Norm Index; the UN sustainable development goals on gender equality; and others are signs of great progress. Global leaders recognize there's much to learn about how we achieve equality, and resources are being dedicated to do so. And I believe, in order to make the matriarchy, we'll all need to educate ourselves on what the research is finding so we can set our goals accordingly.

Exploring the UN Sustainable Development Goals (SDGs) provides a great deal of insight and direction. The SDGs "are the blueprint to achieve a better and more sustainable future by all."[60] In 2015, 193 countries committed to enacting change needed to meet the goals by 2030. The complete list of goals are:

---

60   "Take Action for the Sustainable Development Goals," *United Nations*, accessed September 26, 2020.

1. No Poverty

2. Zero Hunger

3. Good Health and Well-being

4. Quality Education

5. Gender Equality

6. Clean Water and Sanitation

7. Affordable and Clean Energy

8. Decent Work and Economic Growth

9. Industry, Innovation and Infrastructure

10. Reduced Inequality

11. Sustainable Cities and Communities

12. Responsible Consumption and Production

13. Climate Action

14. Life Below Water

15. Life on Land

16. Peace, Justice, and Strong Institutions

17. Partnerships[61]

To see gender equality on this list is a testament to its importance in building a better world. According to the SDGs, in order to achieve global gender equality, we must:

- end discrimination against women and girls;
- end all violence against and exploitation of women;

_____
61 Ibid.

- end female genital mutilation and child marriage;
- value unpaid care and promote shared domestic responsibilities;
- ensure universal access to reproductive health and rights;
- ensure equal access to economic resources, land, and property ownership;
- ensure equal opportunities and participation in leadership;
- promote empowerment through technology;

and

- adopt policies and enforce legislation for gender equality.

It sounds like an excellent framework to me and aligns with many of the puzzle pieces that have emerged so far. It begs the next question:

Five years into the plan, how are we doing?

In June of 2019, Equal Measures 2030 published the inaugural SDG Gender Index to quantify progress against the goals and found that no country in the world is on track to achieve gender equality by 2030.[62] With the index using a scoring measurement of zero to one hundred, with one hundred meaning equality has been achieved, the average score across 129 countries in the index was just 65.7, which is considered a poor result in the scoring system.[63]

Once again, scores across countries are interesting: Twenty-one countries achieved marks of eighty or more,

62 Ford, "Not one single," 2019.

63 Ibid.

with the top performers being Denmark (89.3), Finland (88.8), Sweden (88), Norway (87.7), and the Netherlands (86.8) (there go those Nordics again!). The US ranked at number twenty-eight, with a score of 77.6. The worst performers are Chad (33.4), DR Congo (38.2), Congo (44.0), Yemen (44.7), and Niger (44.9).[64]

There's interesting data underpinning those scores. One particularly concerning finding is more than half of countries scored poorly on the specific targets to eliminate all forms of violence against women and girls, end female genital mutilation and child marriage, ensure universal access to sexual and reproductive healthcare, and uphold women's reproductive rights.

At the current pace of progress, the 2020 Global Gender Gap Report estimates it will take nearly a century to achieve gender equality.[65] And warns, additionally, that progress is fluid, and in addition to accelerating progress, we need to be vigilant about protecting and maintaining what has already been achieved.

"It's clear that even in countries at the top of the index that progress is never guaranteed," said Alison Holder, director of Equal Measures 2030. "We need to guard against countries falling backwards."[66] For instance, when the US makes news about rolling back abortion laws or publicly allows those accused of sexual assault into positions of power, it sends a powerful message to other governments about how developed countries

---

64 Equal Measures 2030, *2019 EM2030 SDG Gender Index,* accessed September 26, 2020.

65 Global Gender Gap Report 2020, 4.

66 Ford, "Not one single," 2019.

prioritize gender equality. Essentially, we are all connected when it comes to achieving equality or advancing women globally. It's not only about enjoying a better
quality of life at home. Rather, making and protecting
progress has a tremendous ripple effect for women
around the globe.

The good news here is there's infrastructure growing to support real progress moving forward. Gender
equality is no longer a grassroots issue. Equal Measures
2030 was created in 2016 to provide women's rights
advocates with the data needed to hold governments
responsible for the SDG commitments, and they will
publish the next set of rankings in 2021 and in regular
intervals until 2030.[67] That these goals exist and are
being measured at all is hope that while gender equality
may not be on track for 2030, rapid change is possible
with effort.

A pivotal point in my research journey came when I
found that in 2018 Equal Measures 2030 partnered with
a research firm to survey more than six hundred gender
advocates on their views on progress toward gender
equality. A few key findings capture what the people
on the front lines of this work are experiencing. Key
indicators include:

- Gender advocates have different perspectives on
  progress based on their own gender, with 55 percent
  of male respondents believing gender equality had
  improved in their country and only 33 percent of
  female respondents believing the same;

67   "Who We Are," Equal Measures 2030, accessed September 26, 2020.

- 49 percent of respondents believe gender equality has neither improved nor worsened but, instead, has remained static for the last five years;

- 91 percent believed collecting data to understand the issues that affect girls and women is not a priority for governments;

70 percent indicated they need greater knowledge of existing data and where to find them in order to more effectively promote gender equality.[68] In addition to experiences and observations, the survey asked these 613 experts to indicate the top themes to be addressed in order to achieve equality. The top four themes indicated were: gender-based violence, sexual and reproductive health and rights, economic empowerment, and education.[69]

While reading and exploring the SDGs and corresponding research, I could see the puzzle underpinning my learning journey starting to take shape. World leaders have deemed gender equality a key goal for our long-term sustainability. A variety of global agencies are tracking and measuring progress. And the people on the front lines are aligned on the top goals.

Four goal areas, to be exact.

It was not lost on me the first thing you do when unboxing a puzzle is to *find the four corners.* I had just found my four corners, and it was time to start filling in the more complicated middle.

---

68 "Advocates Survey 2018," Equal Measures 2030, accessed September 26, 2020.

69 Daniel Caroli, "The Three Biggest Priorities in Relation to Gender Equality," *Tableau Public,* last modified September 24, 2018.

CHAPTER 6:

An Interlude on the Intersectionality of Race and Gender Equality

———

Right now, I should be finishing my chapter on education and starting on my chapter on women's health, both of which you may have already read or be chapters away from. That's the funny thing about book writing. You kind of write all over the place, and then spend painstaking months turning it into a cohesive story.

This chapter, then, is a result of what might be described as "writer's block." Except I don't think it's writer's block, because here I am, clearly writing. Rather, if asked to describe it, I think I'd call it "topic block."

Right now, outside my doors and windows, protests have erupted in more than thirty US cities over the death of George Floyd, an unarmed black man who died after being handcuffed and pinned to the ground by a police officer in Minneapolis, Minnesota, on May 25, 2020. We know the graphic details of this incident due to a viral video, which captures an officer keeping his knee on Floyd's neck for nearly nine minutes while Floyd pleads for his life.

The unrest isn't just about George Floyd's death. On March 13, 2020, Breonna Taylor, a black woman who was an EMT in Louisville, Kentucky, was killed in her apartment, shot at least eight times by police who said they were executing a no-knock search warrant. On February 23, 2020, Ahmaud Arbery, a black man out for a jog in his south Georgia neighborhood, was chased down and shot by a white father and son. No arrests were initially made as local officials cited the men chasing Arbery were acting within Georgia's citizen arrest and self-defense statutes. And on May 27, 2020, as the COVID-19 death toll crossed one hundred thousand people, it was found that nearly 23 percent of reported deaths are African American people, even though African American people make up roughly 13 percent of the US population.[70]

So, why does this all bring me here to this "topic block?" I was realizing my learning journey would be incomplete if I didn't take time to acknowledge movements for gender equality have not necessarily benefitted or included all women. And, in writing this book from the perspective of an educated white woman, I needed to pause and fully own my privileges and biases baked in. Despite my best efforts as a writer and your best efforts as a reader, we will each bring our own biases to this journey. Biases are what make us human, but what will make us better

---

70 Berkeley Jr Lovelace, "As US coronavirus deaths cross 100,000, black Americans bear disproportionate share of fatalities," *CNBC Evolve Spotlight*, May 27, 2020.

is our ability to recognize them and work through them for the benefit of all.

The theory of intersectionality was originally introduced in 1989 by civil rights activist and legal scholar Kimberlé Crenshaw. Today, *Merriam-Webster* defines intersectionality as "the idea that when it comes to thinking about how inequalities persist, categories like gender, race, and class are best understood as overlapping and mutually constitutive rather than isolated and distinct."[71] Truly thoughtful scholars, researchers, leaders, and historians look for the intersection of issues to understand the larger context, and in that larger context, look for bigger solutions.

Putting theory into practice, we can respond to each of the above incidents on a micro-scale, arresting the offenders involved, memorializing each individual lost, and sending aid to the communities of color impacted by the coronavirus. Each of those things is important to do on a micro level, but there is also important work to do on a macro level while understanding the intersectionality of these events to inspire the change needed to build better outcomes.

Applying intersectionality to my journey, the reality is race-bias and gender-bias are born from the same seeds of patriarchy that seek to have power over others and power of exclusion. Until each of us commits, each day, to seeing the biases we were born and raised with and critically analyzing where they come from, we will continue to run into barriers of change. I came to understand if I'm advocating for change rooted in building a society based on inclusion, I have a duty to try and understand

71   *Merriam-Webster*, s.v. "Intersectionality," accessed September 26, 2020.

what inclusion looks like for everyone who has historically been excluded.

Dr. Dorri C. Scott echoed this sentiment when we spoke.
"There is a blindness white woman bring to the table,"
she said. "Awareness is key if we're going to create change
that is good for all women."

I met Dorri after she spoke on a panel about the lessons,
good and bad, we can learn from the suffragists who
pursued the right for women to vote. A cautionary lesson,
Dorri advised, is that while we hail the twentieth amendment as an achievement for all women, it was an achievement that benefitted predominantly white women. Black
women had to fight to be included in movement at all,
and, despite the nineteenth amendment guaranteeing all
citizens the right to vote regardless of sex, it took until
the Voting Rights Act of 1965 to remove the barriers many
black women continued to experience. Arguably today,
there are still many more barriers for women of color to
access their right to vote than for white women.

Without intentionally seeking to include women of all
races, identities, and backgrounds in modern-day movements, Dorri argued, we will continue to limit progress
to some women and not all.

Author Mikki Kendall's book, *Hood Feminism: Notes from
the Women That a Movement Forgot,* provides a tremendous overview of all the issues in which the needs of
black women and white women have not been equally
represented or advanced.

Born and raised in Chicago, Kendall is an army veteran,
a mother, a survivor of domestic violence, a scholar, an

accomplished writer, and, in her words, "a feminist. Mostly."[72] "Mostly," because as Kendall underpins throughout the book, all too often mainstream feminist movements are led and populated predominantly by white women. "For a movement that is meant to represent all women, it often centers on those who already have most of their needs met."[73] For feminist movements to truly be inclusive, she argues, they have "to engage with the obstacles women who are not white face."[74]

Kendall shares personal stories from childhood to present day of poverty, hunger, violence, discrimination, fear, achievement, and reflection. She points out the many places along her journey where the lives of grade school friends took dramatically different turns because of a health crisis, loss of caregivers, food instability, threats to safety, abuse, and more. It is the ever-looming threat of the pitfalls of poverty women in marginalized communities wrestle with daily, and often across multiple generations, that need to be addressed if we're to truly tackle gender equality. Or, as Kendall summarizes so well, "if we're going to say that this is a movement that cares for all women, it has to be one that not only listens to all women, but advocates for their basic needs to be met."[75]

Melinda Gates shares a similar sentiment in her book, *The Moment of Lift: How Empowering Women Changes the World*. Gates, of course, is a wealthy white woman,

72   Mikki Kendall, *Hood Feminism: Notes from the Women That a Movement Forgot* (New York: Viking, 2020), xiv.

73   Ibid, xiii.

74   Ibid, 2.

75   Ibid, 37.

so she doesn't represent the voices of the oppressed. But she uses her book to share stories of the women around the world, giving voice *to* the oppressed, which is one of the best ways to use your privilege.

In the book, Melinda shares the Gates Foundation didn't initially set out to tackle gender equality work. They started out interested in ending world poverty, thinking funding initiatives that addressed food scarcity and disease prevention would achieve it. But, Melinda shares, as she had learned to do in her early days building Microsoft, sometimes the most innovative solutions come when you set aside what you think you know and allow the journey of listening and learning to reveal the path forward. The Gates Foundation would come to find it was impossible to solve hunger without empowering the predominantly female farmers working the land they were still not allowed to own; impossible to improve maternal and newborn health without giving women the knowledge, resources, and ability to control the timing of their pregnancies in the first place; impossible to empower women economically without calculating the value of the burden of unpaid labor they bear.

Melinda's overall message is that everything is connected, and until we stand and be willing to see new things, connect with new people, and practice deep empathy for all humans, the pieces of our collective puzzle will remain scattered, and progress will remain hindered.

Combined, Scott, Kendall, and Gates expanded my lens of what an inclusive movement for gender equality really means and the potential power of its outcomes are even greater than I first imagined. If the matriarchy is rooted in inclusion, it must own that inclusion means ensuring *all* women's needs are met: housing, safety, food security, healthcare, safe and affordable childcare, reproductive justice, equal economic opportunity, and access to education. So, for example, when we work on closing the wage gap, we have to acknowledge that different women experience different gaps. When we figure out how to improve the $0.81 white women earn for every dollar white men earn, we also need to figure out how to improve the $0.75 black, American Indian, Alaska native, and Hispanic women earn.[76] We must recognize that closing the gap for one race doesn't automatically improve outcomes for all races or job levels for that matter. Understanding and incorporating complexity is key.

Today's "topic block" was there because my brain was too busy trying to reconcile the topic I actually needed to write. And that is acknowledging and holding space for all of the bias I bring to this book as a writer and you may feel as a reader. Biases are what makes each of us who we are. But they will hold us back if we let them influence our power. That is patriarchy: the game, competition, or war to use your bias to exclude others.

In the matriarchy, we still have bias, but we see it, we acknowledge it, and we use it to inform how we include those who have previously suffered from it.

Or, as Melinda said it in the (spoiler alert) last sentence of her book, "Others have used their power to push people out. We have to use our power to bring people in. We can't just add one more warring faction. We have to end factions. It's the only way we become whole."[77]

---

76   Pay Scale, *The State of the Gender Pay Gap 2020,* accessed September 26, 2020.

77   Gates, *The Moment of Lift,* 262.

PART TWO

THE PUZZLE MATERIALIZES

In the following section, I'll start each chapter with a list of the "puzzle pieces" we'll explore and end each chapter with a vision statement. In doing so, my hope is to provide some order to the journey as well as be the "visionary futurist" I desire to be.

CHAPTER 7:

Corner #1: Economic Empowerment, Part I

———

THE PUZZLE PIECES: "THE IDEAL WORKER" VS. THE IDEAL PARENT + MOTHERHOOD WAGE PENALTY + WAGE GAP AND WEALTH GAP + DEPENDENCY

Image Source: Catherine Edsell, "I Wanted to Go Out and Change the World But I Couldn't Find a Babysitter," Love Her Wild, February 28, 2017.

Recall the doubt I had early in my writing days when a few women called into question whether gender inequality was even still a thing? I suspect it's easy to think women have access to economic equality, because at first glance we're in lots of workplaces dominating many professions, we own homes and cars, can open lines of credit, and can seemingly access the same economic privileges as anyone else (in developed countries, at least).

On the surface, I am the textbook model of economic equality achieved. Or, perhaps, even the economy of the future, eclipsing my husband in earnings some years. So, I couldn't figure out why in my gut my economic picture always felt a bit heavier, a bit harder, a bit more uncertain and unpredictable.

As I dug into researching this corner, I would feel relieved to find my gut wasn't wrong (it rarely is). There are very real forces working directly against women and their ability to be economically independent. It goes from egregious in developing countries, where women are still treated as property with no earning power of their own, to complex and often hard to see in developed countries, where women graduate college at higher rates, but with more student debt and take longer to pay it off thanks to the wage gap cutting into the overall wealth they can build over a lifetime.

The puzzle pieces on economic equality stack up quickly. Explore the lack of women in leadership and you'll find where it connects to barriers to gaining employment in the first place; the pay-rate at which women enter the workforce; and implicit bias in hiring and evaluating. And then other pieces reveal themselves: like the "motherhood wage penalty," the phenomenon has been documented to show how bearing a disproportionate share of responsibilities at home weighs on the ability to advance or to work at all and how wages stagnate incrementally after the birth of each child.[78] And then you find the wage gap is only the tip of the iceberg; it contributes to a far larger lifetime wealth gap that sets women back in paying off student debt, gives us less to invest in wealth-building strategies and philanthropy, and increases our chances of simply running out of money in old age.

I start with this corner of economic empowerment because it's critically important. I won't go as far as to say it's the most important, because without health, safety, and education, attaining economic independence is very difficult (see how this all connects?). However, what I think is critically important is to acknowledge the barriers to women's economic independence are still *very* real and *very* measurable, all the way from the poorest countries to the richest. Even if you count yourself among the luckiest of women who have access to resources and success, that nagging feeling that somehow this is still *hard* is not imagined. We're still impacted by the gendered decisions of past and present made in economic policy, childcare policy, workplace policy, and business practices. Researching this corner and understanding the barriers ultimately led to what felt like a weight of personal responsibility lifted off of my shoulders. It's not just me, and it's not just you. *The struggle is real*, as they say, so let's explore why.

---

78 Mariko L. Chang, *Shortchanged: Why Women Have Less Wealth and What Can Be Done About It* (Oxford: Oxford University Press, 2012), 65.

THE IDEAL WORKER VS. THE IDEAL PARENT

The image at the start of this chapter is what Catherine Edsell uses to open her 2017 TED Talk titled "How an Adventure with Other Women Could Change Your Life." The quote was on a birthday card her brother gave her that, as Catherine describes, he "had meant it to be funny, but it struck a chord so deep that I burst into tears." Catherine goes on to describe a deep sense of loss for her pre-motherhood career as an expedition leader and losing her sense of self as a young mother.[79] Her talk is about how she channeled her grief to launch the Matriarch Adventure, a guided safari through the Namibian wilderness designed for small groups of women to reconnect with nature, themselves, communities of women who host them along the way, and the matriarchal creatures, like elephants, roaming our planet.[80] In doing so, Catherine says, "I was back. I could stop talking about myself in the past tense."[81]

The quote and Edsell's talk stirred something in me as well. I too felt like my professional life just wasn't the same after the birth of my daughter, despite the fact that I kept working and advancing each year. It felt much harder, the choices more limited, the guilt near bottomless, and the resentment toward my husband growing each time I begged out of work for a childcare obligation while he stayed at the office undisturbed.

It turns out I was feeling the weight of the ideal worker phenomenon. "The ideal worker" is a term used to

79 Catherine Edsell, "How an adventure with other women could change your life," Ted Talks. June 27, 2017, Video, 11:51.

80 Catherine Edsell, "The Matriarch Adventures," *Cathadventure*, accessed on September 26, 2020.

81 Edsell, *How an adventure*.

describe the characteristics of real or perceived performance standards employees are held to. In the US, our
ideal worker is one who is reliably at the office day in
and day out; who comes early and stays late; who doesn't
need pesky accommodations like flex time, parental
leave, or predictable hours; is passionately devoted to
the work and eager to climb the corporate ladder; and,
because of said devotion, will prioritize and deliver on
just about anything the employer needs, like last minute
travel, relocation, or stepping up for additional duties.[82]

Or, as author Bridgid Schulte describes:

> The ideal worker, freed from all home duties,
> devotes himself completely to the workplace.
> He is a face-time warrior, the first one in in the
> morning and the last to leave at night. He is rarely
> sick. Never takes a vacation or brings along work
> if he does. The ideal worker can jump on a plane
> whenever the boss asks because someone else is
> responsible for getting the kids off to school or
> attending the preschool play. In the professional
> work, he is the one who answers e-mails at 3:00
> a.m., willingly relocates whenever and wherever
> the company directs, and pulls all-nighters on
> last-minute projects at a moment's notice. In the
> blue-collar workplace, he is always ready to work
> overtime or a second shift.83

When I first read this quote my gut dropped, because
it was a near perfect description of my husband in the
years his career was advancing quickly. Simultaneously,

82 Brigid Schulte, *Overwhelmed: How to Work, Love, and Play When No One Has the Time* (London: Picador, 2015).

83 Ibid, 77.

it was a description I knew I could never meet since becoming a mom.

In her book, *Overwhelmed: How to Work, Love, and Play When No One Has the Time,* Schulte goes to great lengths to unpack the concept of the ideal worker and how its forces are impacting our workplaces and, by extension, our lives. As proof the phenomenon is real, she shares the findings of a 2011 survey conducted by WFD Consulting that surveyed more than 2,000 organizational leaders around the globe. They found more than three-quarters of bosses "thought the best and most productive workers 'are those without a lot of personal commitments' and more than half believed any employee who was 'committed to their personal/family lives cannot be highly committed to their work.'"[84] She also shares the results of a Cornell University study on caregiver bias in the workplace, which found fathers to be perceived overall as more hirable, promotable, and held to more lenient standards of punctuality. Mothers, on the other hand, seemingly couldn't win on any front; they were viewed as "less competent, less intelligent, and less committed than women without children." They were held to "harsher performance and punctuality standards" and were rated as less promotable.[85]

These qualitative findings play out in quantitative ways. Studies show after controlling for things like education and experience, average pay for mothers drops by 4 percent after the birth of the first child and another 12 percent for each additional child.[86] Further, a 2019 study

---

84   Ibid, 79.

85   Ibid, 80.

86   Chang, *Shortchanged,* 65.

shows even a decade after childbirth, the wage loss has not recovered. In the US, for example, mothers experienced a 40 percent change in salary ten years after the birth of a child.[87] And if you're still not convinced it's the ideal worker phenomenon at play, the study also found even *fathers* in the US experienced a 2 percent change in salary ten years after the birth of a child. Additional indicators show while men and women start entry-level jobs at similar rates (51 percent for men and 48 percent for women), women fail to advance at the same rates as men, with 62 percent men at the management level compared to just 38 percent women, and at the C-Suite level a whopping 78 percent are men compared to only 21 percent women.[88] Assuming men and women earn the same entry level jobs because they have equal skills and experience (and are supposed to have equal opportunities to advance along the way) it stands to reason that becoming a caregiver is in direct conflict with our ideal worker expectations. This results in penalties for all caregivers, but is, as demonstrated, far more severe for women.

It was starting to become clear the ideal worker phenomenon creates a looming bias that can play out consciously as discrimination or unconsciously as culture. The immediate impact of this bias is economic, stifling women's (and parent's) ability to earn, advance, and lead, which, as we would come to learn, is the premier driver of women's wealth gap.

---

87   Scott, *The Double X,* 158.

88   Women in the Workplace, *Lean In,* accessed September 26, 2020.

WAGE GAP + WEALTH GAP = DEPENDENCY

I suspect for most of you the gender wage gap is not a new concept: it's the measured gap between the income of women and men at any given time and place. In the US in 2020, the gap stands at women earning $0.81 for every dollar a man is paid, regardless of job type or worker seniority. When further dis-aggregating the data by race, we find that black, Hispanic and American Indian women earn just $0.75 for every dollar.[89]

On the surface, the wage gap is unfair and frustrating, but not a new concept. And women have steadily been making gains, so some may think the pathway to economic equality is about staying the course. But what is less discussed and far more limiting is the gender wealth gap.

When we look at the wealth gap, we see women only own $0.32 of assets for every dollar a man owns.[90] Quantified another way, women may earn 78 percent of what men do, but only own 36 percent as much wealth. Since wages can change from year to year, wealth is a better overall indicator of long-term economic stability. So, despite gains in closing the wage gap, closing the gender wealth gap will be the true mark of equality.

Wealth dictates the ability to weather changes in income and emergencies, to invest in other assets to build additional wealth, to borrow, to bequeath, and to wield influence in politics and philanthropy. People can have positive and negative wealth, and there are external factors that contribute to both, or what

---

89 Pay Scale.

90 Chang, *Shortchanged,* 2.

author Mariko Lin Chang calls "wealth escalators" and "debt anchors" in her book, *Shortchanged: Why Women Have Less Wealth and What Can Be Done About It.*[91] Chang defines wealth escalators as "the variety of legal, institutional, and societal mechanisms that help some convert income into wealth at a much faster pace than is possible by savings alone."[92] Examples she cites are employer pensions, paid sick and vacation time, health insurance, stock options, favorable tax codes, social security, and unemployment insurance. Debt anchors, on the other hand, Chang defines as "acts to prevent aspiring savers from accessing many of the components of the wealth escalator."[93] For women, these "acts" are generally the acts of discrimination and everyday bias impacting our ability to build wealth. Examples include higher interest rates on credit cards for women or the reduction in benefits that come with part-time work or leaving the workforce entirely—most often done by women who can't meet the ideal worker norms. With fewer or no benefits, more income goes to paying for basic needs instead of building wealth.

What I believe is one of the most interesting findings of Chang's research is even if we close the gender wage gap, the wealth gap will likely persist. Chang reports "for every dollar of income men receive, their wealth increases by an average of $5.73," whereas "for every dollar of income women receive, their wealth increases by an average of only $3.85."[94]

---

91   Ibid, 38.

92   Ibid.

93   Ibid.

94   Chang, *Shortchanged,* 40.

This is largely because of the barriers we face in participating in the modern-day workforce. As of January 2020, women held 50.04 percent of American jobs, but within that statistic are the facts that women still hold the majority of lower paying jobs in service and care taking industries and are more likely to hold part-time jobs that don't come with benefits.[95] And let's not forget women are three times as likely as men to drop out of the workforce entirely to be caretakers.[96] Or the fact two-thirds of student debt is held by women, but with our lower wages and wealth, our loans take longer to repay and accrue more interest.[97] All of these have an impact on the fringe benefits that build wealth: access to pension plans and stock benefits, access to benefits that generally only come with full-time employment, and even the number of income-earning years will eventually determine the social security benefits women are eligible for.

As I was deep in the research on wage and wealth gaps, I remembered to pull back from the details and ask—why does this matter? Why is this not just about equality for the sake of equality, but actually creating a better society for all?

I recalled a common thread of almost everything I had read about gender equality, in rich countries and in poor: the key to stronger societies is reducing dependency and building greater self-sufficiency.

95   Tara Law, "Women Are Now the Majority of the U.S. Workforce—But Working Women Still Face Serious Challenges," *Time*, January 16, 2020.

96   Kim Parker, "Women more than men adjust their careers for family life," *Pew Research Center*, October 1, 2015.

97   Scott, *The Double X*, 159.

There are really only two choices when it comes to one's economic status: independence or dependence. Meeting basic human needs requires resources, so anyone who does not have the tools, resources, or opportunities to build economic independence will always be dependent on someone else for survival. And so, it stands to reason that every barrier a person faces in wage and wealth greatly reduces their ability to be fully independent.

I had a particular awakening on the topic because I had always thought of myself as a pretty independent woman. I did exactly what my parents had raised me to do: get an education, get a job, and provide for myself. But through this lens of dependency, I realized others had influenced many choices in that journey because of my dependency on them. My college choice was influenced by my parents who were chipping in; my job choices were strongly influenced by the health care benefits offered; and later, during my husband's military career, I was constantly reminded of my status as a dependent as I dropped in and out of the workforce to follow his career and relied on his benefits and income during my unemployed gaps. (Plus, in military systems, you are *literally* called a dependent on every form you fill out and often right to your face when you're accessing services on base.)

Now, my upper-middle-class-American-white-lady dependency is dripping with privilege, no doubt. But I suppose the realization I had was that, on the surface, I may look like the model for what achieving economic equality is supposed to look like, but in reality, I was dependent on my parents and banks for my education, and without change my daughter will be too. I was dependent on my husband's income to secure our mortgage, and his employer for health insurance. If I'm here, in all my privilege still technically saddled with dependency, then I am not the model for progress. Only when we fully remove the barriers that increase dependency will we have made real progress.

CHAPTER 8

Corner #1: Economic Empowerment— Matriarchy Style

So how do we do better? Let's return to the original mission: to better understand what a society based on power of inclusion looks like. Knowing the behaviors of developed countries have a way of trickling down around the world, I'm going to dig in on women at work and the countries that have done the most to close their gender wage gap, advance women into leadership, and effectively break down some of the "glass walls" that restrict women.

GENDER EQUITY AT WORK

I met Gender Equity Consultant Lindsey Lathrop-Ryan after she spoke on a panel about how to close the gender wage gap in non-profit leadership. I approached her to share I was inspired by the knowledge she offered, and we hit it off. Lindsey's company, Genclusive, examines gender roles in the workplace and works with both employers and employees to build organizations where there is equal access to leadership, advancement, and pay.

Because Lindsey works both with leaders looking to improve their businesses' practices and with individuals looking to advance their careers, she has a front-row seat to the disparity that often exists between employer goals and actual outcomes for employees. Her anecdotal experiences are backed up by the annual Women in the Workplace report. The 2019 report surveyed 329 organizations employing thirteen million people and surveyed more than 68,500 employees. This report found in the US, for every one hundred men promoted and hired to manager, only seventy-two women are offered the same. And when it comes to quickly addressing disrespectful behavior toward women in the workplace, 50 percent of men believe it's happening while only 32 percent of women do. Finally, only half of employees surveyed think gender diversity is a high priority for their company.[98]

Given her depth of experience working to close gender gaps at work, I reached out to Lindsey and asked her straight out: what does she think it will take to eliminate gender inequality at work? "It's complicated," she said. "It takes a conscious and on-going partnership between employers and employees to achieve success."

She shared the story of a recent client to underpin her point. The client, let's call her Mary, had worked in her office for many years and dreamed of taking on more responsibility in a leadership role, but was having

---

98   "The state of women in corporate America 2019 Report," *Lean In*, last modified September 27, 2020.

trouble advancing. She hired Lindsey to help her figure out what she needed to do to break through, build-skills, address problems, improve, change, and, ideally, advance. As Lindsey got to know Mary, she shared she often baked treats to share in the office. She loved taking care of her co-workers, but worried it left people seeing her as the "office mom" and not a potential leader. Mary really loved taking care of her coworkers and didn't want to have to give those things up, but felt that unless she did, they'd never see her in a different light.

Having done some coaching myself, I could see where this story was headed. Mary was focused on what she needed to change about herself to influence her outcomes. So, I asked Lindsey if it was Mary's job to tamp down a little piece of herself to be seen more like a leader, or the employer's job to address the gender-bias creeping into their decision making? "It's both," Lindsey answered. "Employers can do the work to remove gender bias and promote women, but if women don't see themselves as ready for leadership or have the support they need to be successful efforts will fail. Similarly, we can coach individual women to be ready for leadership and give them the greatest support systems, but if employers don't acknowledge and address their gender-bias, we'll keep bumping our heads on the glass ceiling."

In order to foster more systemic change, Lathrop-Ryan has pioneered an innovative program in the state of Vermont called the Business Peer Exchange. It's a collaborative cohort of employers, business and non-profit leaders, and subject matter experts who commit to a year-long series of exploratory conversations around gender equity and best business practices. This collaborative, community-based approach helps build a common language and system of accountability among peers. It's a place where Lathrop-Ryan and her team share lens-shifting facts and experiences. One fact she shared that shifted my lens is when you disaggregate annual best place to work survey results by gender they often reveal female employees are a lot less satisfied than male employees, but the combined total buoys the results. Similarly, Genclusive's trainings on male allyship have been lens-shifting for participants, often finding men are eager to participate in, but either never would have thought of or were too afraid to ask for. The collaborative model has been so well received and successful in Vermont that Lathrop-Ryan and her business partners are launching a nation-wide virtual model. She believes these collective conversations will make a huge impact in shifting the needle.

It's clear leveling the playing field at work takes a coordinated company-wide effort at a minimum, or even better, a regional approach that keeps cohorts of leaders honest and committed. A few hiring managers sprinkled here and there trying to do the right thing essentially leaves us where we are today, with gains no doubt being made in pay equality and women in leadership, but not the sweeping systems-wide change needed to end gender inequality at work.

IT TAKES TWO TO MAKE A THING GO RIGHT

This corner of the puzzle, perhaps more than anywhere else, is where we need to bring men into the building of this new society. Why? Because they currently hold the wealth and the power. In Forbes's 2020 World's

Billionaires List, nine of the top ten are men.[99] Alice Walton, daughter of Walmart founder Sam Walton, squeezes in at number nine, one place below her *younger brother* Jim.[100] The 2020 list of Fortune 500 companies may have touted a record number of female CEOs, but that number was still just thirty-seven.[101] If we're going to distribute wealth and power more equally, we need people who currently hold it to ally with us both in the office and at home to build a new construct that works for all.

What does partnering together to inspire change look like? It starts by recognizing our current systems are set up to encourage a choose-your-own-adventure system of economic empowerment, which may sound like the epitome of freedom and free-market capitalism. And it might be, if the choose-your-own-adventure for women and men took place on similar terrain. But the reality is, all too often, men (white men, at least) are invited to look out over a broad flat forest with a well-appointed pack, while women start out staring up the side of a cliff with the occasional boulder rolling down, and we're carrying a pack *and* a dependent on our back. The reality is there are far more obstacles baked into our adventure, and those obstacles end up creating dependencies—the very opposite of freedom.

Leaders must work together to see and combat bias that creates more of a glass box than a glass ceiling. Our ideal worker bias influences who we choose to hire, promote,

99   Kerry A Dolan, "The Richest in 2020," *Forbes*, last modified March 18, 2020.

100 Ibid.

101 Emma Hinchliffe, "The number of female CEOs in the Fortune 500 hits an all-time record," *Fortune*, May 18, 2020.

and praise. Led to believe we can "do anything" or "have it all," it's only as we're navigating the biases of our leaders and companies do we constantly run into these hidden barriers that limit our range of motion. In developed countries, the glass walls are women carrying more student debt, dropping out of the workforce at child-bearing age, earning less than men for the same work, being more likely to work jobs that earn less, being passed-over for promotions more often, and being statistically less likely to break into the c-suite. In poor countries and communities, restrictions on women's abilities to open bank accounts, access credit, have cell phones, or get an education literally trap them in a box of dependency, limiting their power, voice, choice, and free-agency in life.

And, as if the box wasn't enough, there's "the glass cliff," a term coined to describe research that finds women who do manage to break into leadership roles are more likely to inherit companies or teams with major challenges and are held to higher standards when it comes to both fixing problems and inspiring growth.[102] An example is Marissa Mayer, who was lauded for smashing through the glass ceiling when she was hired as CEO of Yahoo in 2012. At the time, Yahoo was withering in the shadow of Google, and Mayer was recruited to turn things around. The glass cliff phenomenon finds women are more likely to be recruited to lead struggling companies either because we're viewed as great problem solvers or because fewer men are willing to accept struggling ventures. Five years after accepting the role, Mayer took her plunge off of the glass cliff, being

102 Lydia Dishman, "What is the glass cliff, and why do so many female CEOs fall off it?" *Fast Company*, July 27, 2018.

called on to resign for slow company growth, internal dissent, and plummeting employee morale.[103]

Using part of Mayer's experience as an opportunity to build bias-seeing skills, during her tenure she earned a stone-cold reputation for taking just two weeks of maternity leave with her first child and just four weeks when she later gave birth to twins. Mayer faced criticism as a leader for not modeling a more "traditional" six- to twelve-week maternity leave (for upper middle-class families, at least). However, many fired back on Mayer's behalf that a new dad in her position would have been far from scolded and perhaps even applauded for taking leave at all.

Partnership is about seeing these barriers and differences in standards hidden in plain sight and doing the work to share resources and influence change. It's not just about modeling for men or women specifically, but modeling for all.

WHO CAN WE LEARN FROM?

I returned to the World Economic Forum's Global Gender Gap Index 2020 rankings to see which countries have made the most advances in closing economic gaps between men and women. And once again, I found some expected trends—and some unexpected ones as well.

Iceland ranked number one in the world overall for the narrowest gender gap across all measured categories (economic participation, educational attainment, health and survival, and political empowerment).[104] But when

103 Matt Weinberger and Paige Leskin, "The rise and fall of Marissa Mayer, the once-beloved CEO of Yahoo now pursuing her own venture," *Business Insider,* February 11, 2020.

104 World Economic Forum, 9.

I drilled down to see the rankings for results in just the economic participation category, I was surprised to find Iceland ranked number two behind the country of Benin.[105]

Benin is located in the northeastern part of Africa, narrowly sandwiched between Nigeria and Togo and sharing a northern border with Burkina Faso. It is a small, mostly rural, and very poor country with more than half of its eleven million people living on less than a dollar a day. While I had hoped to uncover some magic nugget of truth on how a very poor country achieves relative economic empowerment across genders, it turns out that, sometimes, poverty just means everyone, regardless of gender, has little economic opportunity.

Alas, in 2019, the World Bank issued Benin a $90 million grant to invest in women and adolescent girls empowerment.[106] The money invests in a wide-range of factors that impact women's economic outcomes in poor countries, including reproductive and maternal healthcare, adolescent health and nutrition services, and education for girls. This strategy aligns with the Gates Foundation; if you want to improve overall outcomes in a country, one of the most effective ways to do it is to invest in empowering women in the economy. Perhaps the best lesson we can learn from Benin is economic empowerment for women takes coordinated strategy and investment, and with both, perhaps an already narrow gap can remain narrow.

While Benin provided a lesson in the importance of planning and investment, functionally there wasn't much to

---

105 Ibid, 12.

106 The World Bank, "Benin Receives $90 Million to Invest in Women and Adolescent Girls' Empowerment to Boost its Human Capital," News release (January 25, 2019).

learn about the secret sauce of closing economic gender gaps in developed countries with existing wide gaps. For that, I turned to number two on the list, Iceland.

Iceland's near non-existent gender gap can be attributed to targeted efforts to close disparities in pay and to make it easy for women to stay in the workforce. Iceland goes above and beyond making it illegal to pay women less than men, but flips the burden of proof from the employee to the employer. Iceland, like many countries, has had equal pay laws on the books since the 1960s. However, those laws still mostly require the employee to find and prove the disparity, often requiring the fortitude to soldier through a lengthy court process to prevail. Recognizing the failures of this structure, in 2018, Iceland passed a law requiring *companies* to regularly prove they pay male and female employees without gender discrimination.[107] Violations are treated with the same seriousness as health and safety violations; they come with hefty fines and requisite corrective action.

The law applies to companies with twenty-five employees or more and requires each organization to submit to something akin to an audit every three years. If evidence of gender-based pay inequality is found, daily fines begin to stack up until rectified. It's worth noting this new law passed a year after female candidates won nearly half of the seats in Iceland's parliament, exemplifying, as we learned with Rwanda, how more women in leadership is an accelerant for improvement.[108]

---

107 Camila Domonoske, "Companies in Iceland Now Required to Demonstrate They Pay Men, Women Fairly," *NPR,* January 3, 2018.

108 Ibid.

This innovative legislation is certainly a piece of the puzzle, but according to Richard Reeves, a senior fellow at the Brookings Institution studying pay gaps around the world, "gender pay equity does not happen by itself."[109] His research finds to truly level the playing field economically for men and women, it will require both organizational and policy change and changing the cultural expectations for men and women at work and at home. "Women continue to 'juggle' family and work life," he says, "which impacts their earnings and advancement. Men are not yet doing the same. The revolution we need now is models of masculinity, not just business models."[110]

Here we turn to Sweden. Also ranked highly on gender equality indexes, Sweden is known for what journalist Irin Carmon describes as "the Dads. Enlightened Swedish dads, with their easy security in their masculinity."[111] She describes these "liberated men" as a byproduct of Sweden's "decades-long war on gender inequality."

Sweden observed early on the influence *maternity* leave had on couples as they were establishing new household routines. As mothers stayed home, they took on the majority of household labor and established primary caregiver routines. These early routines, Iceland found, cemented parenting and household roles almost indefinitely. So, in 1974, it became the first country to implement paid paternity leave with the intention of giving men equal opportunity to learn the new routines

109 Angela Henshall, "What Iceland can teach the world about gender pay gaps," *BBC*, February 10, 2018.

110 Ibid.

111 Irin Carmon, "Can American Men and Women Ever Really Be Equal?" *Time*, September 27, 2018.

of parenting and household chores while they are still being established.[112]

The effect? Today, there's nothing "manly" about choosing to forego this valuable use-or-lose benefit, so men stay home. They learn to pick up more household tasks. They cover doctor's appointments and play dates. And boom, women suddenly have a support system to get back into the workforce, built on top of routines established at home that will make staying in the workforce easier over her career. Layer this on top of affordable universal childcare available since 1971, and you start to see real change. Today, Sweden's birthrates are among the highest in Europe and higher than in the US, all while a higher proportion of Swedish women are in the workforce than American women.[113]

HOW WE TAKE THIS ON

As with each corner of this puzzle, even though the topic feels bigger than everyday life, you only need to pick a piece or two to start a groundswell of change. It's clear that family-friendly policies at work have a significant impact on closing gaps, so look around your workplace and identify opportunities to make organizational change. Perhaps it's advocating for paid parental leave and a culture that celebrates all parents fully using that leave, or child-care stipends, or making available allyship workshops. Share the story of Iceland's pay-equity policies and audits, offer up that in 2020 the PayScale Compensation Best Practice Report found that 38 percent of organizations are doing pay equity analysis, and

112 Ibid.
113 Ibid.

encourage leadership to add your company to the list.[114] Create spaces to talk about gender-bias and the ideal worker phenomenon so we can address whatever unconscious influences they have on how women are evaluated and promoted. Bring a gender lens to daily work, ensuring it's not always women setting up meetings, taking notes, or fetching beverages.

At home, we need to disrupt the cultural norms of women's work versus men's work and the ideal worker. This starts early by ensuring we teach our sons and daughters equally: both should know how to change a tire, and both should know how to cook dinner. Redefine for yourself and for your family how you value the labor that goes into maintaining home and family. It's not the most romantic way to envision marriage, but couples should regularly check-in on the "business" of running the shared household you created. Assign jobs—don't assume one spouse or the other will take on these roles. Regularly talk about what's working or what's not working. Appreciate that this may be a complete departure from how marriage was modeled for you, but unless we commit to breaking household stereotypes and modeling differently, our children will face the same barriers and struggles.

While the above is all a great start, it will still only have a micro-effect on the homes and workplaces we're in. The reality is, it's family-friendly policies and laws that are proven to economically empower women. Take your new-found knowledge of the wealth gap and apply it to the fact the US is one of only two countries in the world

---

114 Pay Scale, *2020 Compensation Best Practices,* accessed September 27, 2020.

with no national policy on paid maternity leave.[115] It's not just annoying, it's economically dis-empowering. If we want to see a macro-effect on all of society and really impact the women who have little power to advocate for themselves, we need to elect leaders who invest in paid parental leave, affordable childcare, and systems that aim to reduce our dependency on each other for basic survival.

THE POWER OF ECONOMIC INCLUSION

If you're still not convinced—more women in the economy simply make good economic sense. Linda Scott's book, *The Double X Economy*, provides three hundred and four pages of proof. A few of her highlights include how the International Monetary fund projects the US GDP would rise by 5 percent if women worked at the same rate as men.[116] This would generate greater tax revenue to reinvest in our country. She also cites key studies by institutions like the UN Development Programme and the World Economic Forum that set out to compare the key components of gender equality with the performance of national economies and are finding "where gender equality was high, national incomes and living standards were also high, but where gender equality was low, countries were trapped in poverty and conflict."[117] Further, it's proven women are more philanthropic and more likely to donate to social services, human services, and environmental causes, whereas men are more likely to

---

115 n.a, "America is the only rich country without a law on paid leave for new parents," *The Economist*, July 18, 2019.

116 Scott, *The Double X Economy*, 9.

117 Ibid, 168.

give to private foundations.[118] Women are more likely to spend money on food, increasing the health of their children and families. And they are more likely to spend to improve the health and general welfare of their children.

We must acknowledge the old systems of economic exclusion are hurting all of us—our women, our families, our children, and our neighbors. Breaking down barriers to economic inclusion is not just good sense, it's literally how we improve the world.

The vision: **A world in which we redefine our ideal worker to reflect a smart worker who espouses balance. A world where we recognize that economically empowering women has a multiplier effect: women earning more and accruing more wealth results in greater investment in humanity, so creating the support systems to enable their economic empowerment are prioritized in policy-making and revered culturally.**

---

118 Chang, *Shortchanged*, 5.

CHAPTER 9

Corner #2: Violence Against Women

THE PUZZLE PIECES: STATISTIC SKIMMING + CHANGING THE AIR WE BREATHE + BUTTERFLIES IN YOUR STOMACH + TEACHING LOVE

"If you can't identify one girl or woman you know who has been a victim of gender based violence, then it's probably the case that no woman has ever trusted you enough to share this with you."[119]

ANGELA HATTERY AND EARL SMITH, AUTHORS OF *GENDER, POWER, AND VIOLENCE: RESPONDING TO SEXUAL AND INTIMATE PARTNER VIOLENCE IN SOCIETY TODAY*

Warning: The following is a lot of data. If your urge is to skim this section, resist. Let this data hit you with the full gravity of the pervasiveness of gender-based violence in our world.

---

119 Angela J. Hattery, *Gender, Power, and Violence: Responding to Sexual and Intimate Partner Violence in Society Today* (Lanham: Rowman & Littlefield Publishers, 2019), 5.

According to the National Coalition Against Domestic Violence, in the US:[120]

- one in three women and one in four men have experienced some form of physical violence by an intimate partner. This includes a range of behaviors not always associated with "domestic violence," and are things like slapping, shoving, and pushing;

- one in four women and one in seven men have been victims of severe physical violence (e.g. beating, burning, or strangling);

- one in five women and one in seventy-one men in the United States has been raped in their lifetime;

- 19.3 million women and 5.1 million men in the United States have been stalked in their lifetime; and

- 72 percent of all murder-suicides involve an intimate partner; 94 percent of the victims of these murder suicides are female.

Those statistics are just for the US. Globally, the UN reports:[121]

- 35 percent of women worldwide have experienced either physical and/or sexual intimate partner violence or sexual violence by a non-partner (not including sexual harassment) at some point in their lives;

- 137 women across the world are killed by a member of their own family every day;

- twelve million girls under eighteen are married each year;

120 Domestic Violence, *National Coalition Against Domestic Violence*, n.d.

121 UN Women, "Facts and Figures: Ending Violence Against Women," last modified November 2019.

- at least two hundred million women and girls aged fifteen to forty-nine have undergone female genital mutilation in the thirty countries with available data. In most of these countries, the majority of girls were cut before age five;

- Approximately fifteen million adolescent girls (aged fifteen to nineteen) worldwide have experienced forced sex (forced sexual intercourse or other sexual acts) at some point in their life;

- 82 percent of women parliamentarians who participated in a study conducted by the Inter-parliamentary Union in thirty-nine countries reported having experienced some form of psychological violence (remarks, gestures, and images of a sexist or humiliating sexual nature made against them or threats and mobbing) while serving their terms;

- The first large-scale research study of violence against women and girls in several areas of South Sudan that have known war and conflict for many years showed 33 percent experienced sexual violence (including rape, attempted rape, or any other unwanted sexual acts) by a non-partner (can include police officers or other armed actors, strangers, or known persons).

It's a lot of data. I know. And if you skimmed that section, I encourage you to go back and read each statistic and let it sink in. For this is my point: As we think about global challenges, it's easy to "skim over" violence against women as a serious and pervasive problem. I suspect the reason more of us aren't disgusted and working to fight this daily is because these statistics don't get the headlines they deserve, or worse, we have been conditioned to accept some of the above behaviors are just "part of being a woman."

I myself am on a tremendous learning curve when it comes to gender-based violence. Around the same time I started this book, I began serving as the Interim President and CEO for Doorways, an organization whose mission is to "create pathways out of homelessness, domestic violence, and sexual assault leading to safe, stable and empowered lives for residents of Arlington, Virginia."[122] Further steepening my learning curve, I had been in this role for just five weeks when the coronavirus pandemic hit. The pandemic triggered global stay-at-home orders, which is like doubling down on danger for anyone experiencing domestic violence, essentially locking them indoors with their abuser and giving abusers increased power and control. As the virus circled the globe, we watched demands on domestic violence services skyrocket, including within our own community.

While I've always been aware that domestic and sexual violence are real and pervasive problems around the world, the experience of working at Doorways and researching this book taught me that awareness of the problem isn't enough. Nor is our tendency to individualize the problem; for example: We feel it's unfortunate for the individuals it happens to, and we should help them, but at the same time we ignore the widespread pervasiveness of violence and the systems built to perpetuate and hide it. If we are to make the matriarchy, our goal must be to eliminate gender-based violence entirely.

122 "Doorways for Women and Families," accessed September 29, 2020.

Culturally, we must demand to treat any violence as unacceptable, inexcusable, intolerable, and *preventable*. Gender-based violence has been around since the dawn of time. As scholars started studying it and activists brought attention to it, it was initially called violence against women. That term is starting to be replaced to acknowledge that men can be victims of violence as well. While it's important to acknowledge gender-based violence can happen to women *and* men, the reality is women are still more likely to be victims than men (if you *still* haven't read the statistics above, now would be a great time). In their book, *Gender, Power, and Violence*, authors Hattery and Smith translate the abundance of data demonstrating gender-based violence predominantly impacts women and remark, "Nearly forty-four million women in the United States have been raped... If forty-four million men in the United States were the victims of these same kinds of violent crimes, it would be a national emergency and resources would be made available to protect men from becoming victims."[123]

While the #MeToo movement has certainly accelerated awareness and action on the topic of sexual violence, Hattery and Smith point out progress overall has been slow in the thirty years since society started talking about these issues, concluding "women and children face as much violence on college campuses, in the military, in prisons, by athletes, by Hollywood producers, by politicians, and in the Catholic Church as they always have." They argue as long as violence and aggression toward women is tolerated and enabled within these key

---

123 Hattery, *Gender, Power, and Violence*, 199.

institutions, we will continue to be a society in which women are victimized.[124]

Having spent the majority of 2020 working at Doorways, I can see so clearly that violence is a very real and present problem right in my own backyard. But it took this front-row seat for me to see that. The pre-2020 me was aware but hadn't taken the time to be as deeply disturbed by the impact as I should be. I write that in hopes of invoking the same awakening in you.

While I believe it goes without saying that ending violence against women is critical to achieving gender equality, it's important to point out how this connects to the rest of the puzzle. Any incident of domestic, sexual, or intimate partner violence creates trauma—trauma that impacts one's sense of safety, trust, self-identity, independence, and more. The impact of domestic violence spans generations as well. Children who are exposed to violence in the home are more likely to be victims of child abuse, to suffer from depression and anxiety, and to be affected by violence as adults—either as victims or perpetrators.[125]

This trauma has the power to change the entire trajectory of one's life, impacting the ability to concentrate or feel safe at school or work; impacting one's long-term health, both physical and mental; impacting stability and self-sufficiency; and so much more.

For those of us lucky enough never to have experienced domestic or sexual violence, we need to appreciate just

124 Ibid, 201.

125 UNICEF, "Behind Closed Doors: The Impact of Domestic Violence on Children," accessed September 29, 2020.

how rare that is and how, in a world that doesn't condone violence against women nearly enough, we all live dangerously close to an incident that can change the entire trajectory of a woman's life and potentially her children's lives. It's a massively important piece of the puzzle.

FROM AWARENESS TO ACTION

This problem, as with many problems that stem from the power-over-others-patriarchy (which creates the incredibly appropriate acronym POOP), seems huge and potentially insurmountable. If total elimination of gender-based violence seems daunting, how do we weave solutions into our everyday lives?

What I have learned on this journey is we have to change the very air we breathe around this subject. Our words and actions (or lack thereof) matter tremendously. We have to open our hearts and minds to learning about gender-based violence so we can empathize with everyone who has been a victim.

It starts by believing survivors. Studies show "96 percent of the time women report a rape it is true, and more than 90 percent of the time the person who raped her has raped or will rape other women."[126] (Meanwhile, RAINN, the largest anti-sexual violence organization in the US, found that just 5.7 percent of reported incidents of rape end in arrest, 0.7 percent result in a felony conviction, and 0.6 percent result in incarceration.)[127]

Our brains are often trained to first wonder if victims were wearing scandalous clothing, or walking alone, or

126 Ibid, 210.

127 RAINN, "The Criminal Justice System: Statistics," accessed September 29, 2020.

had consumed too much alcohol and should have been more careful. This victim-shaming distracts us from putting the full weight of the blame on the person who committed a violent crime. Consider, if you knew you had a 96 percent chance of winning the lottery, you likely wouldn't pause long before deciding to buy a ticket. But how long do you pause before believing a woman when she says she has been raped? We have to retrain our brains to see predators as the sole offenders, and their behaviors must be deeply disdained, aggressively punished, and rehabilitated to prevent re-offending. Survivors are not the offenders.

Providing services to help victims and survivors, a culture that promotes reporting, and more stringent and wide-spread systems for prosecuting offenders are all important, but they all address the problem after a violent and traumatic incident has occurred. To invest the majority of our efforts into reacting and responding to violence after it has occurred is short-sighted. To eliminate gender-based violence, we have to alter the ways in which we train our brains to learn and tolerate it.

Hattery and Smith advocate a true culture shift lies in increasing education and prevention strategies. I was so moved by what I learned via their work that I looked the authors up. I learned that Angie Hattery was the incoming co-director of the Center for the Study of Prevention of Gender Based Violence at the University of Delaware. I took a leap of faith and reached out for her thoughts on the topic of prevention. We had an amazing conversation.

Hattery shared their research has found the factor that "significantly shifted student attitudes about rape culture was completing a course in women and gender studies." They advocate that requiring all students to complete a semester-long course on gender could produce a significant change in culture. That sentiment was echoed by Carla Golden (the professor in women's and gender studies who I introduced back in Chapter 1) when we dug in on her experience teaching gender studies and psychology for thirty years.[128]

Golden shared the majority of her students reported a "life-changing experience" after completing her course, one that caused them to view gender, power, and society in a completely different way. While requiring a gender studies course in college would only impact the part of the population that enrolls, Hattery and Smith advise if a similar in-depth course was included in military training curriculum, we'd very quickly reach a significant portion of the population.

These solutions, however, won't reach people until their late-teens or early-twenties at best. While better than nothing, it leaves plenty of formative years to normalize violence against women. It's not lost on me that this learning and writing journey is heavily influenced by the fact that learning about gender inequity and its root causes was virtually non-existent in my formal education. We have to get comfortable teaching our children about prevention of violence if we are to really turn a corner on ending it.

LET'S TALK ABOUT SEX

As I began to search for the puzzle pieces to inform what it will take to eliminate gender-based violence, I learned a critical component is getting more comfortable

---

128 Hattery, *Gender, Power, and Violence*, 213.

talking to our children about their bodies, about sex, and about gender inequities and power. A preponderance of research reveals age-appropriate conversations on these topics throughout life greatly reduce incidents of gender-based violence.

In Dutch schools, sex-ed begins with a curriculum titled "Kriebels in je buik (Butterflies in Your Stomach)" geared toward elementary-aged children.[129] The curriculum covers a wide-range of topics, including differences between male and female bodies; reproduction; discovering likes and dislikes; setting boundaries; and love, including "how to be kind to your crush." This concept made me think *Awwww* at first. But then I considered how I've legitimately told my daughter sometimes boys torment girls at school because they "like" them. And how, perhaps, I've mistaken the way her face screws up for learning, when really I should see it for the craziness it must sound like. *So, if someone* likes me it*'s okay to show it by being* mean? #Gender-bias-parent-fail.

In 2012, the Dutch education minister mandated all students, country-wide, receive sexuality education on health, tolerance, and assertiveness starting in primary school.[130] Meanwhile, in the US, just twenty-four states and the District of Columbia mandate sex education, and thirty-four states mandate HIV education.[131] Guidelines on how, when, and what is taught vary widely by state, and the details of what exactly is taught are often left up to individual school districts. The CDC recommends sixteen

---

129 Bonnie J. Rough, "How the Dutch Do Sex Ed," *The Atlantic*, August 27, 2018.

130 Ibid.

131 Planned Parenthood, "What's the State of Sex Education in the US," last accessed September 29, 2020.

topics make up essential components of a sex education, but according to the findings of the 2014 CDC School Health Profiles, fewer than half of high schools and only a fifth of middles schools cover all sixteen topics.[132]

Sex education matters in the fight for gender equality, and specifically when it comes to eliminating gender-based violence and violence against women. In 2016, the CDC reported "comprehensive sex education programs have been shown to reduce high risk sexual behavior, a clear factor for sexual violence victimization and perpetration."[133] The Sexuality Information and Education Council of the United States says, "Comprehensive sex education includes age-appropriate, medically accurate information on a broad set of topics related to sexuality including human development, relationships, decision-making, abstinence, contraception, and disease prevention."[134] The key words here are "comprehensive sex education." This means going beyond the basics of rolling condoms onto bananas, handing out feminine hygiene starter kits, and instilling the fear of teen pregnancy in everyone. Nicole Haberland, a researcher with the Population Council, argues "comprehensive" should also include gender and power dynamics. In a 2015 study, she found "teaching about power and gender roles was a consistent predictor of better health outcomes."[135]

Alas, all of the above relies on policy-makers, schools, and teachers getting it right. Many states and educators are

---

132 Ibid.

133 Rough, "How The Dutch," *The Atlantic,* August 27, 2018.

134 Julie Beck, "When Sex Ed Discusses Gender Inequality, Sex Gets Safer," *The Atlantic*, April 27, 2015.

135 Ibid.

beginning the arduous work to create systems change. However, the reality is, if we care about reducing gender-based violence, we can't leave it up to all the room for error within those often biased systems. One of the most powerful ways we can work to eliminate gender-based violence is to ensure these conversations are happening outside of school.

Now, if your heart is in your throat (as mine is, and as my mother's was, and as I'm sure her mother's was before her) when it comes to talking with kids about the minefield that is sex, gender, power, and specifically gender-based violence, it's okay. Many of us have been conditioned for years to think talking about sex, good or bad, is verboten. But the making of the matriarchy means building new and better things, and in this case, it starts with learning about the tools and resources available to have these conversations.

An interesting resource I found is called "Voices Against Violence," published by the World Association of Girl Guides and Girl Scouts and UN Women.[136] The co-educational curriculum was designed for age groups ranging from five to twenty-five and was developed with input from young people. Housed at UNWomen.org, the curriculum includes a handbook for peer educators to aid in delivering age-appropriate sessions and activities.[137]

Again, with age-appropriateness being key, "Voices Against Violence" provides tools for young groups to start out with storytelling and games that prompt them

---

136 World Association of Girl Guides and Girl Scouts and UN Women, "Voices Against Violence," UN Women, 2013.

137 Ibid.

to think about gender bias and stereotypes. For older kids, there are tools for organizing poster competitions, visiting and volunteering with local shelters, or developing community-based campaigns to bring awareness and education around violence against girls and women. What's beautiful about this program is that it's peer-driven and group-oriented, allowing young minds to drive the work and create common knowledge with their peers, bringing a collective awareness to a whole group instead of a one-by-one approach. Plus, it allows us nervous parents to partner with our kids in this process; to serve as facilitators instead of the sole-source truth speakers we're terrified to be. We all get to be brave together.

We can also commit to learning and teaching about love as more than just a feeling of "butterflies in your stomach." It's important to develop a language around healthy and unhealthy relationships and the often small warning signals that are precursors to more serious domestic and sexual violence.

Love and relationships are the cornerstones of our lives, and yet we train very little for them. Katie Hood, CEO of One Love, makes a similar point in her 2019 TED talk titled "The difference between healthy and unhealthy love."[138] One Love was founded in honor of Yeardley Love, a University of Virginia lacrosse player who in 2010, just three weeks shy of her college graduation, was beaten to death by her boyfriend. Her gruesome death shocked her family, and it was only in hindsight

138 Katie Hood, "The difference between healthy and unhealthy love," Ted Talks, 2019.

they realized there were warning signs that Yeardley, a strong, smart, empowered woman, was the victim of a very unhealthy relationship.[139]

One Love's mission is to "educate young people about healthy and unhealthy relationships, empowering them to identify and avoid abuse and learn how to love better."[140] They engage students through films, conversation, peer-to-peer discussions and workshops, and offer frameworks to enable students to spread these teachings through online communities. Getting started on their website is beautifully simple, walking visitors through Relationships 101: ten signs of a healthy relationship and ten signs of an unhealthy relationship.[141] In case you don't have the time to make the jump to JoinOneLove.org and learn those signs, the ten signs of an unhealthy relationship are intensity, possessiveness, manipulation, isolation, sabotage, belittling, guilting, volatility, deflecting responsibility, and betrayal. If any of those words spark anything in you about your relationship or of someone you love, please, visit the site and educate yourself.

Education, conversation, and changing the words we breathe around domestic and sexual violence is the way forward, and there are plenty of resources out there if you commit to looking, learning, and taking action.

WHAT ELSE?

Gender-based violence has been written about extensively, and there's plenty more to learn outside the pages of this book. Reading Hattery and Smith's book changed

139 One Love, "About Yeardley," accessed September 29, 2020.

140 One Love, accessed September 29, 2020.

141 One Love, "Relationships 101," accessed September 29, 2020.

my view on power and violence in institutions—and how if we start there, we could impact so much of society quickly. Volumes have been written over the course of decades on how damaging porn is to perceptions of what sex really is. Steinem devotes an entire chapter titled "Erotica vs. Porn" in *Outrageous Acts and Everyday Rebellions.* As I read her detailed descriptions of the pervasiveness of the porn industry, I was certain I was a reading a recent update. Alas, the end of the chapter revealed the content has remained mostly unchanged in the 1977, 1978, 1993 and 2018 versions. And frankly, the porn problem is only getting worse with the invention of the internet. Porn is more accessible than ever, especially to young people, and is shaping ideas of gender roles and sexuality in often aggressive and demeaning ways. As Steinem advocates, we must learn and teach about the differences between porn (power-based) and erotica (pleasure-based); strikingly similar to patriarchy (power over others), and matriarchy (power of inclusion).

Get comfortable talking, learning, and listening about sexuality. It's human nature, literally survival of our species, and not a taboo topic to hide or fill with shame. Secrecy and shame enable predators to perpetrate sexual violence and abuse, because victims are too afraid and ashamed to come forward. The #MeToo movement proved that a groundswell of change can happen quickly if we all start talking and believing.

Much of this chapter has skipped over the more gruesome global realities of sexual and domestic violence. Sexual violence against women in war torn countries is pervasive. In fact, as the Women Peace and Security

Index found, the level of political unrest in a country can be directly correlated to rates of violence against women. The 2019 report found "a 1 percentage point increase in the share of women experiencing current intimate partner violence is associated with a 1.4 percent increase in organized violence."[142] I believe it's important to recognize that sexual violence against women and children can be used as a weapon of war, and work must be done to help those survivors and build prevention strategies. I've chosen to focus this chapter predominantly on the work needed in the US because that's where it feels like there's the most opportunity for readers to change behaviors and create impact. And it's important to recognize that leaders around the world turn to superpower countries for signaling on what is acceptable behavior. So, it is incredibly important both for our own societies and the ripple effect around the world that we hold our leaders accountable, model gender-balanced behaviors, and vehemently reject sexual violence as acceptable.

The vision: **Dominance expressed through physical, mental, or emotional abuse is culturally unacceptable. Gender-equality education starts early and is a common-core subject like math or reading. Any violence or abuse against women is treated an egregious offense. We believe survivors, without question. Punishment for gender-based crimes is aggressive.**

---

142 GIWPS, "Women, Peace, and Security Index," accessed September 22, 2020.

CHAPTER 10:

Corner #3: Education

THE PUZZLE PIECES: EQUALITY ACHIEVED(?) + BIAS BEGINS EARLY + ILL-EQUIPPED FOR THE FUTURE ECONOMY + PTAS TO POLICY

It's easy to overlook education. In the 2020 Global Gender Gap Report produced by the World Economic Forum, data in the Educational Attainment sub index shows 96.1 percent of the global gender gap has been closed (i.e., the average educational attainment for boys and girls globally is almost equal). The 2020 Index reports thirty-five countries have achieved "full-parity" in this sub index, though results vary once you drill down on the data, with varying degrees of parity at the primary, secondary, and tertiary levels (to include, girls graduating from tertiary education at *higher* levels than boys: 40.6 percent of women compared to 35.6 percent of men globally attend higher education).[143]

With the gender gap in education declared all but closed and *more* women than men graduating college, can we

---

143 Global Gender Gap Report 2020, 11.

declare just one corner of gender equality achieved, pop some bubbly, and move on?

Sadly, no. In fact, it was a shocking personal experience regarding gender in education that kicked off my journey writing this book. Thanks to stats like the above and the optics of most schools, I had been cruising along believing gender parity was largely achieved in education. With equality largely achieved in access to education, I assumed the quality of a girl's educational experience had improved as well. I couldn't have been more wrong.

When my daughter was in second grade, she came home tasked to prepare for a "wax museum" event. For this project, students needed to choose a historical figure to research so they could dress up and emulate this person in the "museum" parents would visit one afternoon. The assignment came home with a list of ten historical figures to choose from. They were:

Christopher Columbus
Benjamin Franklin
Abraham Lincoln
George Washington Carver
Helen Keller
Thurgood Marshall
Rosa Parks
Jackie Robinson
Cesar Chavez
Martin Luther King, Jr.

In the context of homework and the mountains of paperwork that come home each night, nothing stuck out to me at first. My daughter had circled her top three choices:

Helen Keller, Rosa Parks, and Jackie Robinson. As I tried to understand those choices, it suddenly jumped off the page she had circled what she thought were women's names. Which then caused me to see the stark contrast you may have seen earlier than I did given the context of this book: of the ten choices, only two are women.

Becoming frustrated, I responded how many of us do nowadays. I snapped a photo of the list with my daughter's circled choices, posted it to Facebook with a caption that can best be summarize as "WTF?" and moved on to making dinner.

Checking on that post a few hours later, I discovered many other second grade moms had noticed and were equally frustrated. I also learned other schools in our district were doing the same wax museum activity and had not sent home a list of pre-determined choices at all, giving students the opportunity to choose whomever they liked.

I conjured a mental image of what my attending this "wax museum" was going to look like: a room with a handful of George Washingtons and Abraham Lincolns, and a sprinkling of Cesar Chavezes and Thurgood Marshalls mixed in with thirty Helen Kellers and twenty Rosa Parks. I imagined my daughter looking around that room and thinking, *Lots of choices for boys, few choices for girls.*

I wasn't okay with it.

I decided to write an email to the school principal and include the signatures of the moms who had responded to my post, asking (politely!) that the list be modified to include more women or removed from the activity entirely to let the kids choose any historical figure they were interested in. It seemed a simple enough problem with a simple enough answer.

I'll never forget the way my gut clenched when I read the principal's email response. She informed me the list was sourced directly from the state of Virginia's second grade curriculum, and that while the teachers (all women!) recognized the imbalance and were themselves frustrated, it was *the* curriculum, so they thought it best to move forward with the activity as planned.

That email stirred all sorts of feelings in me. The fact that it was *in* the curriculum was offensive enough, but the added fact that the women hired to teach this curriculum felt powerless at best, apathetic at worst, to change it really blew my mind. There was evidence of teachers in other schools nearby who had thrown this list out the window for this activity. Why hadn't our teachers thrown it out? If our teachers hadn't thrown it out, how many other teachers and schools were teaching this same limited list? If the list looks like this in second grade, what does it look like in the rest of the K-12 state-wide curriculum? If the list looks like this in the state of Virginia, what does it look like in Alabama? Are the majority of students still being taught that if you want to make the history books, you've got a better shot if you're a man? Or worse, that all our societies have achieved is predominantly thanks to men?

Clearly, my brain was spinning with many questions, but the K-12 question dogged me the most. If this was my daughter's prescribed experience in second grade, was it possible she was at the beginning of years of gender-imbalanced curriculum? I decided I needed to know.

I hired an enterprising young woman I found on Fiverr to do the first review of the entire K-12 history and social studies curriculum in the state of Virginia and highlight every reference to a proper name of a man or a woman. Then we counted up those references and found male historical figures were cited as part of the curriculum 1,008 times, and female historical figures were cited directly in the curriculum just 105 times, meaning women make up just 9.4 percent of the conversation in Virginia's history and social science K-12 curriculum. I noticed in this initial pass she had counted mentions of "Martin Luther King, Jr. Day" or "Columbus Day" in the men's headcount. Not wanting to inflate the numbers, we passed back through and eliminated those, coming up with a new total of just 10.2 percent of the curriculum citing female historical figures. Finally, on my own, I wanted to understand if multiple mentions of the same name (i.e.: the fact that George Washington is mentioned just about every freaking year of the curriculum) was skewing the numbers. Even when eliminating duplicate mentions, I could still only get to about 13 percent of the curriculum citing female figures to study.

Reading the entire curriculum allowed me to come to a sobering conclusion: the education my daughter is receiving in history and social studies is not that different from the one I received thirty years ago. A significant part of my writing journey has been grappling with how little women's history I was exposed to until I was an adult and sought it out myself. I felt short-changed by my educators and the system but figured surely someone would have updated the curriculum since then. Here I was, being shown how dead wrong I was.

It's here I recalled a 2017 study published when my daughter was in kindergarten. The study found six-year-old girls are less likely than six-year-old boys to believe they are "really, really, smart."[144] Further, the research reports by age six, girls begin to avoid certain activities they believe are only for "really, really smart" children—i.e., boys.[145]

So, we know our girls are doubting their smarts and abilities by kindergarten (ugh), and then we have a curriculum that fails to expose them to all of the brave and brilliant women they should aspire to be like (double ugh). How do we expect our children to grow up and lead the world differently if we aren't giving them the opportunity to see it differently?

THE DEVIL IS IN THE DETAILS

While boys and girls may be enrolling and graduating at similar rates, the experiences they have and their eventual outcomes still point to a great deal of gender inequity.

Joseph Cimpian and his colleague Sarah Lubienski have studied gender achievement for more than a decade. And they believe "as soon as girls enter school, they are

---

144 Valerie Strauss, "It's 2017, and girls still don't think they are as smart as boys, research shows," *Washington Post*, February 14, 2017.

145 Lin Bian, Sarah-Jane Leslie, and Andrei Cimpian, "Gender stereotypes about intellectual ability emerge early and influence children's interests," AAAS Science, 6323, no. 355 (2017): 389-391, accessed May 16, 2020.

underestimated."[146] This is backed up by the data collected in their nationally representative Early Childhood Longitudinal Study, which found "no average gender gap in math test scores existed when boys and girls entered kindergarten, but a gap of nearly 0.25 standard deviations developed in favor of boys by around second or third grade."[147]

They found this gap has much to do with the gender bias teachers often unknowingly apply between their male and female students. Specifically, they found "when faced with a boy and a girl of the same race and socio-economic status who performed equally well on math tests and whom the teacher rated equally well in behaving and engaging with school, *the teacher rated the boy as more mathematically able*—an alarming pattern that replicated in a separate data set collected over a decade later."[148]

If we view this disparity through the lens of the long-term impact on women in STEM related fields, this early bias is the equivalent of driving the shovel into the ground and unearthing the first scoop of dirt in what, over a lifetime, will eventually become a very big hole for women to climb out of. In fact, Cimpian and Lubienski suspect if teachers didn't apply this gender-bias in evaluating the math competencies of girls and boys, the overall gender gap in math-related fields would likely be substantially smaller.

What may start as unintentional gender-bias in elementary school evolves into a much larger problem

---

146 Joseph Cimpian, "How our education system undermines gender equity," Brookings, April 23, 2018.

147 Ibid.

148 Ibid.

throughout society, and fast. By higher education, women who pursue career paths in math and sciences are met with continued bias and aggression leveled by their teachers and classmates. In 2012, Yale published a study demonstrating that physicists, chemists, and biologist were likely to view "young male scientists more favorably than a woman with the same qualifications."[149] This held true whether the scientist surveyed was female or male (i.e., even female scientists favored males).

This consistent bias throughout a woman's education is leaving women ill-equipped to compete in the fields that will dominate the future of our economy. The 2018 World Economic Forum "Future of Jobs Report" projected through 2022, 133 million jobs stand to be *gained* in emerging fields around data and AI, while as many as seventy-five million jobs will likely be *lost* in fields like data entry, accounting, and administrative functions.[150] In this new economy, workers with "disruptive technical skills" will prevail; things like cloud computing, engineering, data and AI, and product development.[151] These skills are all rooted in math competencies, which we're setting girls up for a disadvantage in starting by second grade.

I was gutted to reconcile I had been so blind to how my daughter's brain was being shaped intentionally in underwhelming curriculum and unintentionally through bias. This was an example in equality versus equity. Boys and

---

149 Eileen Pollack, "Why are there still so few women in science," *The New York Times*, October 6, 2013.

150 World Economic Forum, "The Future of Jobs Report," accessed October 3, 2020.

151 Jon Younger, "The Future Of Work According To WEF Davos 2020: 5 Minute Summary," *Forbes*, February 1, 2020.

girls may have equal access to education but lack equity in the quality of their experience. We must do better.

CREATING SOME CHEMISTRY

For any parent who has ever sat at the kitchen table and tried to coax their child through a subject they are struggling with, it's time to recognize it may have less to do with their skills and more to do with subliminal messages impacting their confidence before they ever sat down. It's not just about exposing girls to STEM activities, it's about helping them through their frustrations and reminding them, maybe excessively, they are good at this.

It was here I recalled a headline I saved on my desktop for a long time. I saved it largely because I loved the image that went along with it. It's an image of a very beautiful woman on a big glitzy stage. Her perfectly coiffed hair and makeup glimmer behind her safety googles, and her gorgeously tanned legs peek out from under her long white lab coat. Three giant multi-colored foam explosions are erupting all over the table and floor behind her, creating disarray where perfection is expected to reign supreme. The headline accompanying this colorful and exhilarating image reads: "Miss America 2020 goes to Virginia biochemist Camille Schrier after on-stage science experiment."[152]

I know my daughter would find just about everything cool about this image. The explosions. The *mess*. The fancy stages. The pretty girl. The continuation of gender-equity

---

152 "Virginia biochemist is crowned Miss America after performing onstage science experiment," *CBS News,* December 20, 2019.

work we face in education is ensuring our young girls have plenty of images like these to connect to as they envision their dreams and commit to the courage it will take to pursue them.

But this brings us back to the similar challenge we saw in economic empowerment. Is it up to our girls to develop stronger courage of conviction to pursue their dreams through an educational system that is slowly nudging them down conventional and expected paths, or is it up to us to change the systems?

In case you haven't noticed by now, I believe the latter.

Addressing gender-bias in our teachers and curriculum is particularly interesting to me. Growing up with a mother who was an elementary school teacher for over thirty years and a grandmother who was a middle-school science teacher, I can see how, collectively, they influenced the lives and minds of *thousands* of children across their careers. It's teachers who have the platform to influence future generations in a broad and sweeping way, so it seems we could make a tremendous impact by equipping our teachers to see and avoid the remaining pitfalls of gender inequality in education.

Now, I can hear all of you who are teachers saying, "Seriously? Another thing for us to learn and be responsible for? We are already overwhelmed and overburdened with *all the things*." And I get that, I really do. One of my very best friends, who in all her kindness, compassion, and patience was simply born to be an elementary educator, has dropped out of the profession citing spending more time on paperwork and compliance than actually doing what she loved, which was teaching. I've heard her ridiculous compliance stories first-hand. But hear me out.

We know from the section on violence against women that adding training here and there is rarely effective at creating major shifts in culture and a critical shift we could make would be requiring a gender studies class as part of core requirements. In theory, this would include students who go on to be teachers, so a solution might start there.

But that change would be a huge undertaking, and its reach will only be limited to the new classes of students training to be teachers, which might lead to *my daughter* having the same curriculum shock with her kids thirty years from now. So that means we need both long- and short-term solutions.

In searching for ideas around more immediate solutions, I connected with Catherine Bailey, founder and creator of ThinkOrBlue.com. Catherine, an attorney, gender policy advocate, feminist, and mom, started the blog, resource center, and website after taking her infant daughter to the park one day, dressed in navy blue, and noticed how differently people talked to her baby in more strong and confident tones when they thought she was a boy. It was then she committed to the work of breaking down gender stereotypes when it comes to children.

Catherine pointed me to a 2018 BBC documentary called "No More Boys and Girls." In the documentary, Dr. Javid Abdelmoneim conducted an experiment in a first-grade classroom in the UK that was designed to measure gender roles and stereotypes among the children.[153]

Catherine shared Dr. Abdelmoneim found everything we've already discussed here: girls lack confidence while

---

153 David Abdelmoneim, "No more boys and girls: Can our kids go gender free?" BBC. n.d., Video.

boys overestimate themselves; boys have trouble with emotions; and children start believing boys are smarter around first grade. So, he worked with the teachers to introduce solutions, which included: ensuring inclusive spaces and resources (at this school that included over-hauling the library to include more books with female lead characters and removing the gender separated coat area); helping kids see they are equally strong (in this case, girls and boys participated in the carnival game that measures strength where you swing the hammer with enough force to ring the bell. Before playing, children were asked to guess where they would land. Of course, girls underestimated themselves, and the students got to see that boys and girls could hit the bell equally and that, sometimes, girls were stronger than boys too); diminish-ing teacher bias (in this case, all of the students names were put into a basket, and when the teacher needed to call on someone, they simply picked a name); and using examples to defy gender stereotypes in professions (i.e., students drew pictures of mechanics and dancers [all men for the first, and all women for the second], and then brought a female mechanic and a male dancer in to help breakdown the reality of that stereotype.)

In her review of the documentary, Bailey noticed and recommended even more opportunities. Recess, for example, is often very segregated, whether by accident or design. Bailey suggests finding ways to design facil-itated physical activities that normalize strength and physical ability regardless of gender. And, she points out, there was a running undercurrent of girls being given the opportunity to act more like boys, when in reality, we need to bend the lenses so that children can just *be and love who they are*—strong, kind, compassionate, smart, athletic, or whatever they may be.[154]

As I thought back to where I began on this corner, I pondered how to impact change. Having spent my fair share of time serving on the PTA, I suspect there's a role for PTAs to play in tackling gender bias in schools. Yes, that means the impact would be limited only to certain schools, likely the more privileged ones with well-organized PTAs. But if we can influence even a handful of schools and the handfuls of teachers and children roaming their hallways, then we can begin to influence the future those children will tolerate and create.

PTAs build amazing partnerships with school administrators and teachers and leverage their power of fundraising to drive additional resources to schools. Our PTA already drives resources for library enhancements, technology, and enrichment activities, and we probably have room to tackle headier subjects than school picnics, carnivals, and spirit-wear. What if we could partner with teachers to build a school community rooted in how important it is to break down the gender barriers that start forming by first grade and influence literally the rest of their lives? It could be as simple as some parents coming together and creating more content for teachers to pull from during Women's History Month (bulletin boards and such), or volunteering to come in and visit classrooms if you *are* a female mechanic or male dancer. Or it could be bigger, like investing in training or supporting higher-level policy change efforts at the local, state, and federal levels.

---

154 Catherine Bailey, "No More Boys and Girls? A Series Review About Gender Stereotypes in Schools," Think or Blue, August 21, 2020.

In this corner, there really are no shortage of options to impact change. It can be as simple as the language you use to encourage your child who is struggling with homework or certain subjects. Or volunteering to visit your school and share your profession, or raising this with your PTA and brainstorming opportunities to act, or electing school board members who have this in their agenda to take on.

If you want to go even bigger, check out the Patsy T. Mink and Louise M. Slaughter Gender Equity in Education Act (GEEA) of 2019. The act is designed to double down on Title IX and help address gender discrimination in all areas of education by providing additional training and resources, establishing an Office of Gender Equity in the US Department of Education, and authorizing competitive grants to K-12 schools, colleges, local education agencies, and states to invest in gender equity work.[155] The American Association of University Women (AAUW) makes it *so* simple to urge your congress person to support that bill in the "two-minute activist" section of their website. There, you can see all of the legislation that addresses gender inequities, click through a form, find your congress person, send a pre-designed note, and boom, done.

Taking on the topic of creating gender equity in education must go beyond a single school, district, or state. We need to ensure that educating the next generation about gender equality is not just a privilege of affluence. I love there are books like *Good Night Stories for Rebel Girls* and even a *Women Who Dared* building block set I saw in a

---

155 AAUW, "Support the Gender Equity in Education Act," accessed October 3, 2020.

bougee bookstore, but at their $20 and $64 respective price points, we can't count on every little girl having access to these educational tools.

If we are to achieve gender equality, our public education system needs to give every student the opportunity to learn without the weight of gender bias bearing down on them. They need to learn that achievement by men and women has been happening for a long time, and they will experience even more opportunity than ever before. We need to raise children who believe they are all equally strong, smart, and compassionate so they can build a future society that embraces those same qualities for all.

As far as my personal story with gender in education goes, I am exploring what goes into proposing curriculum change in the state of Virginia and understanding what the process looks like so I can assemble an action plan. Once I figure that out and hopefully inspire change in my own backyard, perhaps I'll rally and move on to other states. Or perhaps if you're feeling inspired, you can download your state's curriculum and let me know what you find.

The vision: **Gender has no influence over quality of, or access to, education. All students have equal access, opportunity, and expectations. History curriculum is intentionally updated to be more inclusive and representative of women. Gender-bias in education is recognized and addressed by faculty and administrators.**

CHAPTER 11:

Corner #4: Women's Health

———

THE PUZZLE PIECES: HEALTH AS THE FOUNDATION OF LIFE + OUTCOMES AND ECONOMICS + THE FUTURE OF THE HUMAN RACE + MAKING MOTHERHOOD ATTRACTIVE AGAIN + INVESTING IN WOMEN'S HEALTH

Admittedly, I wrestled to write this corner more than any of the others. In each of the other corners I had personal experiences that helped me relate to what I was learning. When it comes to health challenges and inequities, however, I am woefully inexperienced. I've always had health insurance and thankfully no major incidents in which to experience the difficulties of navigating coverage. I had perfect attendance for all four years of high school. I had no trouble getting pregnant with my daughter, and a healthy and easy pregnancy and birth followed. My newborn daughter scored a ten out of ten on the APGAR (the test given to newborns to measure things like oxygenation, pulse, reflexes, and alertness to determine the health of a baby at birth). I once had a dentist call me "dentally boring." It's probably the only time in my life I've been incredibly grateful to be called boring. I've not had to wage war with my health, health systems, or the health of my family to truly experience systemic inequities I know exist.

My closest connection is all of the women in my life whose journeys have been *very* different. There's the friend who "accidentally" gave birth to her first child without pain medication because the machines weren't registering her contractions and hospital staff assured this first-time mom if contractions weren't registering, they couldn't be nearly as painful as she was complaining they were. Only when her doctors were prepping her for surgery after hours of labor and "no progress" did she wind up feeling the urge to push and deliver naturally. Or the neighbor who, after being told she couldn't get pregnant, was very nearly convinced by her male OB-GYN she might have a cancerous tumor growing in her uterus. Turns out, after a lot of unnecessary stress, the required pregnancy test before a procedure revealed she was nearly three months pregnant with her son. Or there's the other neighbor who experienced, as many moms do, the rush to kick new moms out of the hospital after birth. I myself was given forty-eight hours after c-section before my insurance would stop covering my stay. Thankfully, I experienced no major issues. My neighbor, on the other hand, found herself back in the hospital just a few days later battling very serious and dangerous issues with her blood pressure. Thankfully, she turned out okay, but since then she battles crippling health anxiety, fearful that missing the smallest thing could spell certain death.

That these are all pregnancy related stories is probably a reflection of my age and stage in life. My mother has no shortage of stories from her teaching days about female colleagues who have practically dropped dead from heart attacks, or who lost all hope navigating the limitations of their health coverage in retirement, or who stopped going to preventative care appointments because they were too expensive. I'm reminded of a woman I worked with in my early twenties who seemed to have countless medical challenges, keeping her out of work frequently. She was young and kind and sweet and self-deprecating about it all, which led one of our co-workers to lovingly nickname her "Brokedown Mountain" (the movie Broke-back Mountain was popular at the time).

To do this chapter justice, it's important I recognize the fact that my exceptionally healthy experience (for which I am profoundly grateful) is the exception, not the rule. It is by sheer luck and a lot of privilege I haven't had to grapple with health experiences that routinely set women around the world behind. In reality, women are far more likely to be living like "brokedown mountains."

This feels almost too basic to say, but health is the foundation of life. It underpins *everything*. If you're not in good health, it impacts your relationships, your work, your happiness, your prosperity, your life expectancy, and, well, *everything*. I can hear you saying right now, "Yes, yes, yes, I *know* that. Get on with it." But as I've asked you to do in other chapters, pause here and get rooted in this thought: without your health, nothing else matters. If you don't have a healthy body to be in, then just *being* gets very difficult.

It's this root that drives the importance and complexity of this corner of the puzzle. If health is the root of being, then a system that treats genders differently toys with our very ability to be—to be strong, to be well, to be empowered, to be supported, and to be confident that we have what we need to go on *being*.

Only in the last few decades has studying women and health become more prevalent. For the majority of human history, only men were recruited for clinical studies and findings were assumed to represent everyone. But low and behold, once they started including women, inequities were laid bare. For instance, a range of studies on pain from 1989 to 2008 found men are twice as likely to be given narcotics for pain; women are less likely to be admitted when reporting things like chest pain, and even when they are admitted, men wait an average of forty-nine minutes while women wait an average of sixty-five.[156]

Many studies have shown women interact with systems of health care more than men. They utilize it for their own care and often—as primary caregivers for both offspring and elders—interact with the system as they navigate caring for others.[157] But, for a long time, it was harder and more expensive for women to secure health care coverage, and as recently as 2008 there were still random gender-based restrictions in play, like the seven US states that allowed private insurers to deny coverage to women who had been victims of domestic violence.

156 Zoanne Clack, "Women's health concerns are dismissed more, studied less," *National Geographic*, December 17, 2019.

157 Klea D. Bertakis, "Gender Differences in the Utilization of Health Care Services," *J Fam Pract*, 49, no. 2 (2000): 147, accessed September 29, 2020.

The Affordable Care Act of 2010 addressed many gender-based inequalities in health coverage, but overall, women's health is still lagging far behind in effectiveness and outcomes.[158]

I've spent most of this book advocating for gender equality. However, as I dug in to research this corner of the puzzle, it became clear I can't advocate for equality in health. Because by the very nature of what our bodies are designed to do, males and females can never be equal in the roles we play in sustaining the human race. Yes, of course, it takes elements of male and female biology to create human life. But try as you might to argue roles and responsibilities after sperm and egg join, for humans at least, only females can provide the forty weeks of gestation needed to create a new human. And, even if *you* choose not to be a mother, you still came from one, and her health at the time of your birth and throughout your childhood impacts *your* health outcomes.

So, it's here I'm going to stray from advocating for equality and argue that if you care about the continuation and proliferation of the human race, our health systems must *prioritize* women's health. To be clear, I'm not advocating females should be in peak physical condition while males wither away, but rather I'm arguing if we *prioritize* women's health, it will have a ripple effect through our roles as mothers of new humans and caretakers and partners of existing humans and improve the whole of human health.

There is plenty of research to underpin this idea. According to the Partnership for Maternal, Newborn, and Child Health, every dollar invested in reproductive, maternal,

158 Family Violence Prevention and Services Program, "The Affordable Care Act and Women's Health," last modified December 2013.

newborn, and child health generates $20 in benefits across society.[159] Further, research on correlations between a country's health and wealth find that a 10 percent increase in life expectancy generates a 0.4 percent increase in economic growth. Studies that have compared outcomes for children over time find "children born after the advent of federally funded family-planning programs lived in households with higher annual incomes and were 5 percent less likely to live in poverty, 15 percent less likely to live in households receiving public assistance, and 4 percent less likely to have a single parent."[160]

As I was thinking this through and how far it might creep from the topicality of this book, it hit me this is squarely within where we started examining matriarchies. These societies hold in high honor and esteem the role women play in human existence, and there's historical evidence that it's the way the whole world may have operated at one time. It's here I ask us to return to what we have learned about the power of prioritizing women and advocate the future priority of the health of women while also ensuring we have full control, knowledge, and decision-making authority when it comes to our health.

SOMETHING FOR EVERYONE, I PROMISE

Melinda Gates holds her Catholic upbringing and continued faith central to who she is. And she talks openly in her book, *The Moment of Lift*, of her struggle to reconcile the teachings of her church on family planning with the

---

159 The Partnership for Maternal, Newborn, and Child Health, "The Economic Benefits of Investing in Women's and Children's Health," last modified in 2013.

160 Andrea Flynn, "The Economic Case for Funding Planned Parenthood," *The Atlantic,* September 17, 2015.

The Power and Promise of Prioritizing Women

realities of what she has witnessed around the world, both in data and first-person storytelling.

She cites a study from the 1970s that tracked outcomes for families across Bangladesh over the course of twenty years. In the study, half of the women in participating villages were given access to contraceptives, while the other half were not. At the end of the study, women who were given contraceptives were healthier, their children were better nourished, their families had more wealth, the women earned higher wages, and children had more schooling.[161]

She shares the story of Meena, a woman she met in Mozambique. Gates was visiting Meena, who had recently delivered her infant son in a new clinic, to ask her about her experience and how it compared to giving birth to her first son, then two, at home. She was prepared for a conversation about how having access to the clinic was a dramatic improvement for the health and well-being of mom and baby, which Meena confirmed. She wasn't prepared for Meena's response when she asked if she wanted to have more children.

Meena shared that they were very poor. Her husband worked hard, but she still worried about her ability to provide for the two children she had, let alone more. Gates describes "reeling" when Meena said, "The only hope I have for this child's future is if you'll take him home with you."[162] It was in this moment Gates realized "the pain of giving her babies away was less than the pain of keeping them."[163]

---

161 Gates, *The Moment of Lift*, 18.

162 Ibid, 56.

163 Ibid.

It was Meena's story, and many more like hers, that drove Gates to take a stance very different from the teachings of her Catholic faith on family planning. She realized "when women can decide whether and when to have children, it saves lives, promotes health, expands education, and creates prosperity—no matter what country in the world you're talking about."[164] The Gates Foundation, in its quest to end poverty, end starvation, lower maternal and infant mortality, and in general reduce suffering around the world, realized it needed to prioritize empowering women to manage their health and reproductive *journey* to be successful.

"The reasons are simple," Gates writes. "When the women were able to time and space their pregnancies, they were more likely to advance their education, earn an income, raise healthy children, and have the time and money to give each child the food, care, and education needed to thrive."

I share Gates' story to invite you to set aside any existing biases you may have when it comes to overlapping women's health with politics or personal beliefs. Women are responsible for the proliferation of the human race, and as I dug deeper on data and stories, it became clear to see the best outcomes for society (and frankly, the world) are born out of empowering women in their health decisions.

WOMEN'S HEALTH AND THE FUTURE OF THE WORLD

You may recall earlier in the book I shared the statistic that nearly half of the countries in the world are producing

---
164 Ibid, 87.

too few children to sustain their populations. But what about the other half? Who *is* producing enough children?[165]

Turns out, the world has gone topsy-turvy, and not in a good way. According to the 2020 World Population Review, the African country of Niger tops the list with an average of 7.153 children per woman. Somalia comes in next at 6.123, followed by the Democratic Republic of Congo, Mali, and Chad.[166] I could keep going, but the list is best summed up with this startling statistic: Of the thirty-five most fertile countries in the world, "more than two-thirds are among the most fragile states in the world."[167]

Meanwhile, fertility rates have been falling steadily for years in the most stable and developed places in the world. Taiwan has the lowest fertility rate at 1.218 children per woman, followed by Moldova and Portugal. Across all of Europe no country breaks 2.0.[168] The US stands at 1.779 births per woman. When you zoom in further on birthrates across economic status, in the US we are a microcosm of the global phenomenon, with the highest birthrates in families with less than $10,000 in income per year. The rate steadily shrinks as household income rises.[169]

---

165 Scott, *The Double X,* 145.

166 World Population Review, "Total Fertility Rate 2020," accessed September 29, 2020.

167 Scott, *The Double X,* 149.

168 World Population Review, "Total Fertility Rate 2020," accessed September 29, 2020.

169 Erin Duffin, "Birth rate by family income in the US 2017," *Statista,* July 16, 2020.

The fertility rate needed to maintain a society's population size is 2.1 children per woman, and globally in 2020, our combined average stands at 2.448 births per woman.[170] But it's clear the over-performance of the world's poorest countries is compensating for the under-performance of the most developed. Allowing these trends to continue is essentially resigning ourselves to a planet where the majority of humans are born into poverty. A multitude of studies have shown that being born into poverty can have long-term negative impacts on physical health, mental health, educational attainment, employment rates, and life expectancy.[171] If these trends in birthrates persist, the future of the human race looks pretty bleak.

Learning this data was a stark moment of realization for me that I am a contributing factor to these statistics. Having hated every minute of my pregnancy and feeling like I lost myself completely in the pressures of motherhood, I am a one-and-done woman. I thought it was good enough I fulfilled my societal obligations of producing offspring, until I read this data and learned that couples who produce less than two children haven't even done the work of replacing *themselves.* Guilty as charged.

Fans of the Hulu drama *The Handmaid's Tale* may be experiencing ominous foreshadowing at the moment. (It gets even worse when you learn the series is based on a book by the same title, originally published in 1985 by author Margaret Atwood as a dystopian fiction novel.) In both versions, a key contributing factor to

170 World Population Review, "Total Fertility Rate."

171 Priyanka Boghani, "How Poverty Can Follow Children Into Adulthood," *PBS Frontline*, November 22, 2017.

the creation of the oppressive and practically medieval society of Gilead is that birthrates had fallen near the point-of-no-return, so fertile women were captured and kept as handmaids for breeding.[172]

That's certainly the extreme end of the scale I hope no developed society will consider to increase their birthrates. However, there are still plenty of people who look back to the healthy fertility of the 1950s and '60s (the US peaked at 3.582 in 1958, fell below replacement rate in 1973, and has been declining since) and believe returning to those more traditional roles is the solution.[173] However, I think it's fair to assume we'd have to go through some sort of Handmaids-esque type takeover to expect women to participate in that complete reversal.

Rather, might the way to solving our human survival woes lie in investing in systems that enable women to feel empowered in the proliferation of humankind by make birthing and raising children affordable and attractive instead of the present status life-and-death gauntlet for your body, your brain, and your bank account? And by acknowledging that access to birth control is just as important a piece of this equation?

LET'S MAKE MOTHERHOOD ATTRACTIVE AGAIN

It can be argued motherhood is a dangerous, thankless job with serious economic ramifications. Consider, in the US, the maternal mortality rate is seventeen deaths per

172 Margaret Atwood, *The Handmaid's Tale.* (Toronto: McClelland and Stewart, 1985).

173 Macrotrends, "US Fertility Rate 1950-2020," accessed September 29, 2020.

one hundred thousand live births (forty-one deaths per one hundred thousand live births for black women).[174] The average cost of giving birth in the US is $4,500, and that's *with* insurance.[175] Assuming you manage to survive and afford pregnancy and childbirth, the CDC finds one in eight women report experiencing postpartum depression.[176] Further, a 2020 study designed to inform the WHO postnatal guide found postnatal care is woefully understudied, underfunded, and overlooked once the baby is born.[177]

If you manage to survive those odds, the USDA reports in the US, it costs a middle-income family $233,610 to provide food, shelter, and necessities for a child from birth to seventeen, and that doesn't include college.[178] Add in what we learned back in the economic corner of the puzzle about the motherhood wage penalty and motherhood starts to look pretty darn daunting. It certainly begins to explain why fewer and fewer educated women are voluntarily stepping up to the task and why many women in impoverished places desire so deeply to be able to have control over the number of children they have.

Many countries are tackling their population concerns with policies designed to make women's health safer

174 Maternal Health Task Force, "Maternal Health in the United States," accessed September 29, 2020.

175 Olga Khazan, "The High Cost of Having a Baby in America," *The Atlantic*, January 6, 2020.

176 Centers for Disease Control and Prevention, "Depression Among Women," last modified May 14, 2020.

177 Finlayson, Kenneth, "What matters to women in the postnatal period: A meta-synthesis of qualitative studies," *PLoS ONE*, 15, no. 4 (2020): e0231415.

178 Mark Lino, "The Cost of Raising a Child," US Department of Agriculture, February 18, 2020.

and caring for children more palatable. In 2007, Russia launched a "maternity capital" payment of £5,800 ($7,600) for families with two or more children. Italy launched a similar €800 payment per couple per birth. But, according to Anne Gauthier, a professor of comparative family studies at the University of Groningen in the Netherlands, these one-off baby bonuses "usually have very little impact on the fertility rate."[179]

It turns out the countries seeing the most success in raising birthrates are those who recognize the full-spectrum of challenges and commitment motherhood presents and have chosen to prioritize the health of women through this lens of motherhood. Scandinavian countries top the list, with Sweden posting the regional high of 1.8 children per woman, up from a low of 1.5 in 1998.[180] With a maternal mortality rate of just four per one hundred thousand live births, a monthly allowance of 1,573 krona ($167) per child, and generous leave policies allowing for up to 480 days of paid parental leave over the life of the child, not only has Sweden raised their birthrates, but the European Commission has found that "female and maternal employment rates are among the highest in the EU, and child poverty is among the lowest."[181]

I also found an interesting movement with roots in the past and present: the motherhood pension. In 1911, Illinois became the first state in the US to pass a statewide mothers' pension law.[182] These pensions set out to

179 "How do countries fight falling birth rates?" *BBC News*, January 15, 2020.

180 Macrotrends, "Sweden Fertility Rate 1950-2020," accessed September 29, 2020.

181 "How do countries fight."

182 Joanne L. Goodwin, "Mothers' Pensions," Encyclopedia of Chicago, last accessed September 29, 2020.

provide a subsidy to mothers with children in households without the income of an adult male. These policies in Illinois and other states that followed were more aid for the impoverished than a recognition of the hardship bearing children can bring. However, this led to the discovery of a new movement as a more literal motherhood pension payment. In 2019, European consumer group Which? began calling for a "£2,000 pension top-up, from the government, for new mums."[183] It's designed to acknowledge that mothers end up saving up to 40 percent less for retirement than their male peers and up to £15,000 less than their female peers due to time taken out of the workforce to care for children. The £2,000 ($2,655 US) payout at the time of birth works to help close this gap when invested in a retirement savings account and allowed to grow over time.

Bearing children is dangerous, challenging, and not the most lucrative job. At the same time, it is rewarding, fulfilling, and essential to society. These are the same framework for many jobs we award pensions: firefighting, military service, teaching, and police. These are the jobs we consider to be critical to our society, so why not add parenthood to the list?

IT'S NOT ALL ABOUT MOTHERHOOD

I've chosen to focus largely on motherhood so far because in any given year more than half of women aged fifteen to forty-four will give birth.[184] But it's critical not to let

183 Serina Sandhu, "Mothers 'should be given £2,000 pension top-up for having to take time off work to have children,'" *INews*, June 3, 2019, last modified Oct 8, 2020.

184 Centers for Disease Control and Prevention, "Births and Natality," last modified January 20, 2017.

this chapter be entirely about motherhood, because women's health is not solely about maternal health. Heart disease kills more women than men annually and is the leading cause of death for women; 80 percent of people with autoimmune diseases are women; and the World Health Organization reports that "depression is the most common mental health problem for women, and suicide a leading cause of death for women under sixty."[185] We've got plenty of challenges to tackle in addition to maternal health.

It was becoming clear investing specifically in women's health is a critical factor for progress. It was only in 1993 that clinical trials began to include women. That means women's health is decades, perhaps lifetimes, behind in medical research and innovation.

Amy Millman, president of Springboard Enterprises, couldn't agree more. She co-founded Springboard in 2000 to funnel investment capital to high-growth technology and life science companies led by women. Millman sees health through the numbers: The annual cost of managing patients with ovarian cancer in the US is $612 million; uterine fibroid tumors costs the US $5.9 to 34.4 billion annually; and the unrecognized and inadequate treatment of cardiovascular disease in women contributes to the $1 trillion increase in costs projected by 2035.[186] In addition to Springboard, Millman recently launched the Women's Health Innovation Coalition, designed to focus

185 Centers for Disease Control and Prevention, "Leading Causes of Death—Females—All races and origins—United States, 2017," last modified November 20, 2019; World Health Organization, "Ten top issues for women's health," accessed September 29, 2020.

186 Geri Stengel, "Market Ripe For Disruption Lacks Investment," *Forbes*, July 8, 2020.

on gender-specific health, which by 2027 is projected to represent a $47.8 billion market.[187]

Millman and the pioneers Springboard and the Coalition support reflect the belief that a rapid investment in women's health, led by women who can call upon a combination of professional training *and* lived experience, will change the future of women's health.

An example is Aspira Women's Health, led by Valerie Palmieri, whose previous company, LifeCycle Laboratories, was funded by Springboard. Aspira is innovating in ovarian cancer, a cancer with a mortality rate greater than 50 percent, which when compared to the 2 to 5 percent mortality rates of prostate and testicular cancers points out the dramatic differences in gender-based cancer outcomes. Aspira is using algorithms to assess ovarian cancer risk from a blood test, which means signs of cancer can be caught in phase one or two where survival rates are 70 to 80 percent. Palmieri reports, "We can detect ovarian cancer risk with 98 percent sensitivity... while the standard of care only catches 50 to 60 percent of early-stage disease."[188]

Standard of care to future of care accelerated by investment in companies led by women with a commitment to improving women's health. That sounds like some critical pieces of the women's heath puzzle to me.

FINAL THOUGHTS

Swapping harrowing health-care stories is the fodder of just about every gathering of women I've ever been a part of. We take turns one-upping each other on the

187 Ibid.
188 Ibid.

nightmares of fertility, not being believed about pain, working through illness, being mansplained to by doctors, and more. My editor suggested this section needed more of those personal stories, but I respect you too much to bore you with more of what you likely hear all the time.

Rather, I hope I've taken an all-too-often politicized topic and made it approachable, interesting, and piqued your curiosity. It's clear that commiserating to each other, while cathartic, won't put an end to our health care woes. Instead, we must recognize that as the health of women suffers, the health of society suffers. Improving women's health has the power to improve the health of entire societies, creating healthier future generations, improving poverty and nourishment, reducing healthcare costs in the long run, and creating better long-term outcomes for all.

The vision: **A world where the quality of women's health is prioritized as the root of the health of all humans.**

CHAPTER 12

Corner #5: Women in Leadership

———

THE PUZZLE PIECES: POWER VS. LEADERSHIP + PROOF IN PANDEMIC + PROOF IN PARLIAMENT + BIAS TO BLAME

Okay, I know the average puzzle has four corners, but the making of the matriarchy is not your average puzzle. Perhaps it's more of a Rubik's Cube or custom die-cut variety. Puzzle analogies aside, I couldn't get through this exploration without talking specifically about the importance of women in leadership. And here's where I'll stress not in *power,* but in leadership. As this learning journey progressed, it became more and more clear that the *patriarchy is about power* and the *matriarchy is about leadership.* In fact, as I visualized where "women in leadership" belonged in our puzzle, it seemed it should be a funny round-shaped piece encircling the "matriarchy" piece at the center, one that essentially ties all of the other pieces to the core. But then it occurred to me, perhaps women in leadership *is* the matriarchy piece in the center of a fully assembled puzzle.

If the goal is a more inclusive and equitable world, then my findings demonstrated over and over again that progress toward equality accelerates when there are more women in leadership roles. And while I've tried to provide examples of ways we can all act as individuals to advance gender equality, the reality is our individual actions are dwarfed by policies and systemic structures that are failing us; ones leaders have the ability to change. Women in leadership, at the local, state, federal, and global levels, are critical to progress.

Recall the lingo; Merriam Webster defines matriarchy as "a family, group, or state governed by a matriarch (a woman who rules or dominates a family, group, or state)."[189] But in our new version of the matriarchy, let's strip *rules* and *dominates* (power words) from that definition and update it simply to be about a woman who leads.

Merriam Webster defines leadership as:[190]

1: the office or position of a leader.

2: capacity to lead.

3: the act or an instance of leading.

A position. A capacity. An action. Not power or control. Leadership, not power, is the hallmark of the matriarchy.

WOMEN'S LEADERSHIP EFFECTIVENESS IS RIGHT IN FRONT OF OUR (MASKED) FACES

When I set out on this equality exploration, I had no idea the bulk of my writing would take place during the biggest pandemic the world has seen since the 1918 Spanish

189 "Matriarchy."

190 *Merriam-Webster*, s.v. "Leadership," accessed October 3, 2020.

flu. As a firm believer the universe puts us right where we're meant to be, this was a stroke of luck for a few reasons: 1) I had way more time to hunker down in my comfy pants and write; 2) it was the first time the world has had a common enemy of this scale while there were also twenty-one incumbent female heads of state;[191] and 3) there was a ton of new pandemic data to explore through the gender-lens. And the stories of success were stacking up.

When Taiwan's President, Tsai Ing-wen, heard about a mysterious new virus in the Chinese city of Wuhan in December of 2019, she immediately ordered all planes arriving from Wuhan to be inspected. When other Asian countries were in the peak of the virus, Taiwan had just 395 recorded cases and six deaths, and they had enough leftover personal protective gear that they exported it out to help other countries.

German Chancellor Angela Merkel, with her doctorate in quantum chemistry, took early action on the testing front. Even when there were relatively few cases, Germany began wide-spread testing and quarantine orders that limited the spread of the disease. With the virus under control, Merkel deployed their Air Force planes to transport patients from the harder-hit parts of Europe to Germany for care and treatment.

Slovakia's President, Zuzana Čaputová, implemented one of the quickest nationwide lockdowns just eight days after the country had their first confirmed case and has consistently held the spot for lowest death totals in

---

191 Council on Foreign Relations, "Women's Power Index," last modified September 18, 2020.

Europe, at just seven per one million people as of August 2020. By contrast, in August the US had 580 deaths per one million people.[192]

At thirty-seven years old, Jacinda Ardern became the youngest prime minister New Zealand has had in 150 years and their youngest female prime minister ever. In 2018, she was the first world leader in thirty years to have a child while in office. She was, by all accounts, a badass female leader pre-pandemic. As coronavirus began to spread around the globe, Ardern took bold preventative action that shut down tourism and imposed a month-long country-wide lockdown. Her clear and coordinated leadership delivered a country-wide text message that read, *Act as if you have COVID-19, This will save lives. Let's all do our bit to unite against COVID-19.*[193] New Zealand would become the envy of the world when, after just five weeks of strict lockdown, reopening began after there were no new positive cases in seventeen days. They continued on to reach more than one hundred days with no community spread.[194]

In the Nordic region, four of the five included countries are led by women. Finland has the world's youngest leader, Prime Minister Sanna Marin. At just thirty-four-years old, she has an 85 percent approval rating among Finns for her handling of the pandemic, containing the impact to just sixty-one deaths per one million people

---

192 Worldometer, "COVID-19 Coronavirus Pandemic Live Update," last updated November 16, 2020.

193 Anna Fifield, "New Zealand Isn't Just Flattening the Curve, It's Squashing It," *Washington Post*, April 7, 2020.

194 Julia Hollingsworth, "How New Zealand went 100 days with no community coronavirus transmission," *CNN*, August 10, 2020.

as of April 2020.[195] (Even in November of 2020, Finland's death rate had only risen to seventy-five deaths per one million people).[196] In Iceland, Prime Minister Katrín Jackobsdóttir implemented large-scale randomized testing that not only saved lives in Iceland, but gave the world the valuable insight that half of all people who tested positive for the virus were asymptomatic. Demonstrating this isn't just regional happenstance, Sweden (that one Nordic Country not run by a woman) suffered when Prime Minister Stefan Löfven refused to impose a lockdown and kept schools and businesses open. At the time of writing in November of 2020, Sweden's death rate stands at six hundred ninety-eight deaths per one million people, far higher than its Nordic neighbors.[197]

Perhaps one of my favorite findings are the quotes of Prime Minister Silveria Jacobs from the tiny Caribbean island of Sint Maarten who told her citizens via video, "Simply. Stop. Moving," and "if you do not have the type of bread you like in your house, eat crackers. If you do not have bread, eat cereal. Eat oats. Eat... sardines."[198] It's amusing to me how Jacob's guidance sound much like directions I've issued to my daughter over the years: *Stop moving. Eat what we have. Don't be selfish.* Could it be that skills honed while managing hangry toddlers

195 Leta H. Fincher, "Women leaders are doing a disproportionately great job at handling the pandemic. So why aren't there more of them?" *CNN*, April 16, 2020.

196 Worldometer, "COVID-19 Coronavirus Pandemic Live Update," last updated November 16, 2020.

197 Ibid.

198 Jon Henley and Eleanor A. Roy, "Are female leaders more successful at managing the coronavirus crisis?" *The Guardian*, April 25, 2020.

are particularly useful when governing hangry citizens during a global pandemic? Perhaps.

It's the leadership characteristics of reckless risk-taking, overconfidence, and hubris proven more common in men that have been dangerous and lethal during the coronavirus pandemic. Examples like Belarus, where President Alexander Lukashenko "encouraged citizens to drink vodka and visit the sauna at least twice a week to stay healthy."[199] Or where UK Prime Minister Boris Johnson initially downplayed the severity of the crisis and refused to introduce restrictions on social gatherings. He boldly declared the virus would not stop him from shaking hands. That overconfidence led to Johnson testing positive for the virus and eventually spending three nights in the ICU fighting the infection. Similarly, in the US, an early October event hosted by President Donald Trump at the White House, void of masks and social distancing, would eventually be deemed a "superspreader" event, linking to at least twenty-five government officials testing positive in the following weeks.[200] And, in arguably the biggest leadership mistake of all, Chinese President Xi Jinping allowed five million people to leave Wuhan (the city with the first-known case in the world) before it went on lockdown.

Now, this isn't to say female leaders are flat-out winning against the pandemic while male leaders are flat-out failing. South Korea's male president, Moon Jae-in, also squashed the curve by instituting wide-spread testing.

199 Sam Meredith, "Belarus' president dismisses coronavirus risk, encourages citizens to drink vodka and visit saunas," *CNBC,* March 31, 2020.

200 Fincher, "Women leaders."

But by and large the countries keeping their infection and death rates down are calling on compassion, empathy, strong social supports, and collaboration to do so. All traits of leadership, not power.

While women succeeding in leadership is certainly not a new concept, this is perhaps the first time in history we can examine, on a global scale, outcomes against the same challenge through a gender lens. The data certainly points to trends that can't be ignored, and the number of stories focusing on women leaders and their handling of the pandemic is perhaps the best publicity campaign in history for the power of women's leadership. A silver-lining of COVID-19 may be an ability to see and believe that more women in leadership is a good thing.

Writer Joan Michelson points this out in her March 2020 article for *Forbes* titled, "What's the Surprising Leadership Lesson in the COVID-19 Crisis?" In it, she cites a 2017 Harvard Business Review study that proved qualities associated with female leadership styles: collaboration, self-control, authenticity, trust building, teamwork, and responsibility, to name a few, are historically undervalued. She writes, "Because women have not had access to levers of authority, access to the funding, and other resources, and the instant credibility that men have had, they have found creative, resourceful ways to get things done."[201] As I read the article, I wasn't "surprised" by this leadership lesson at all. We're born out of decades, nay, millenniums of thinking creatively, pulling people together, and overcoming obstacles.

201 Joan Michelson, "What's The Surprising Leadership Lesson In The COVID-19 Crisis?" *Forbes,* March 28, 2020.

What's perhaps "surprising" is we've seen this trend before but still can't use it as concrete evidence to squash our gender bias. In the aftermath of the 2008 financial crisis, several reports found banks and countries with higher representation of women in leadership suffered less from the economic crisis. It famously caused the then head of the International Monetary Fund (IMF) Christine Lagarde to state, "If Lehman Brothers had been Lehman Sisters, today's economic crisis clearly would look quite different."[202]

Will this time be different? One of the memes circling social media during the COVID-19 shutdowns reads, "Our elders were called to war to save lives. We are being called to sit on the couch to save theirs. We can do this." The oldest of those elders are the remaining survivors of the "greatest generation," commonly defined as those who witnessed and survived the frivolity and excess of the 1920s followed by the pain of the Great Depression in the 1930s and the epic global crisis that was WWII that left eighty-five million people dead. I wasn't there, so I can't say if our modern-day global crisis feels similar to the early 1900s. But could this be an opportunity to birth the "next greatest generation?"

We didn't quite get it right after WWII. Prior to the war, women were mostly homemakers or, at best, secretaries, receptionists, or department store clerks. But when men went off to war in droves, it's estimated that up to six million women responded to the call of Rosie the Riveter and joined the civilian work force to keep factories running and more. However, when men returned from war, women

---

202 Tomas Chamorro-Premuzic, "Are Women Better at Managing the Covid-19 Pandemic?" *Forbes*, April 10, 2020.

were expected to return to homemaking. If they managed to keep their jobs they were often demoted.[203] While this time of empowerment for women surely helped to fuel future waves of feminism in the 1960s and 1970s, it was also a tremendous missed opportunity for rapid advancement. I mention this time as a cautionary tale I hope we avoid in the aftermath of this modern-day leadership lesson. We are seeing clearly how women's leadership skills are very, *very* valuable. We can't allow to bury or forget these examples. Having women in leadership matters.

LEADERSHIP OUTSIDE OF CRISIS

As fascinating as it is to explore the effectiveness of women's leadership in times of crisis, we can't let the lesson be to call on women to take charge *only when everything has gone to shit.* Though, lord knows, that's a role we're quite accustomed to playing in our daily lives.

Instead, the crux of the importance of women in leadership as we work toward equality is to examine evidence of how much equality advances when women are in the lead. First, it's helpful to understand where in the world women hold a majority in parliament. According to global data on national parliaments, on Oct 1, 2020, the top ten countries for the percentage of women in parliament are:[204]

1. Rwanda: 61.3 percent

2. Cuba: 53.2 percent

3. Bolivia: 53.1 percent

203 The National WWII Museum. "History At a Glance: Women in World War II," accessed December 6, 2020.

204 IPU Parline, "Monthly ranking of women in national parliaments," last modified October 1, 2020.

4. United Arab Emirates (UAE): 50 percent

5. Mexico: 48.2 percent

6. Nicaragua: 47.3 percent

7. Sweden: 47 percent

8. Andorra: 46.4 percent

9. Finland: 46 percent

10. Costa Rica: 45.6 percent

How do these countries compare to their rankings and advances in the Women Peace and Security Index findings? Rwanda gained fifteen places on the index from 2017 to 2019, and Bolivia gained thirteen places. Finland and Sweden both place in the top ten overall in the rankings. Many of the others, while not necessarily making significant enough gains to improve their overall position, did make significant gains in important areas. Nicaragua, for example, went from 14.1 percent to 24.8 percent of women aged fifteen and older participating in the economy in just those two years.[205]

On a more local scale, I was witnessing evidence of women in leadership creating rapid progress in my home state of Virginia. The 2020 General Assembly has a record high of forty-one female legislators—thirty delegates and eleven senators. Women chair seven of the fourteen committees in the House and four out of eleven in the state senate. And there's the first female speaker of the House of Delegates, Eileen Filler-Corn, at the helm.[206]

---

205 Council on Foreign Relations, "Women's Power Index."

206 Robert McCartney, "Virgina's Year of the Woman produces historic package of liberal legislation," *Washington Post,* March 1, 2020.

The impact of more women in leadership roles has been swift in Virginia. The legislature approved the federal Equal Rights Amendment, becoming the critical thirty-eighth state needed to ratify the amendment and make it eligible for inclusion as the twenty-eighth Amendment to the Constitution (and yes, protection from discrimination on the basis of sex is not yet a promise of the US Constitution).[207] The legislature also passed meaningful anti-discrimination protections in the Virginia Values Act, new protections for pregnant workers in the Pregnant Workers Fairness Act, rolled back restrictions on abortion, and began requiring schools to provide tampons or pads for menstruating girls (this is important, because data shows girls are more likely to miss school if they don't have access to feminine hygiene products).[208]

But for those of you wondering if more women in leadership just makes life better for only women, never fear, studies show it makes life better for *everyone.* In 2019, researchers in Canada set out to understand the impacts more women in leadership have on public health. This was after Prime Minister Justin Trudeau formed the first gender-balanced cabinet in Canadian history in 2015, ensuring half of his closest advisers were women.

Their findings? The big one is mortality rates tend to decline. Reviewing data and leadership trends from 1976 to 2009, they found that women in government increased from 4.2 percent to 25.9 percent, while in the same period mortality declined 37.5 percent. With this finding, they

207 Nicole Tortoriello, "Four major wins for gender equity in virginia's 2020 legislative session," *ACLU Virginia,* May 8, 2020.

208 Amelia F. Knisely, "Teen girls are missing school because they don't have access to feminine hygiene products," *Tennessean,* August 14, 2018.

acknowledged decreased mortality is not *solely* a result of women in leadership, so they controlled for other factors and re-ran the results. And the hypothesis held more women in government advances population health. They even controlled for parties in power to ensure the trends weren't just about a more caring legislature in general. Ideology wasn't at play. The number of women elected to government was.[209]

The researchers found there are four types of government spending that have a direct impact on lowering mortality rates: medical care, preventive care, other social services, and post-secondary education. And that women are more likely to legislate to invest in these areas and use their collaborative leadership styles to achieve bi-partisan success.[210]

Women in leadership beyond elected office matters too. A 2012 study out of the University of California at Berkeley found companies with more women on the boards demonstrate better business practices when it comes to the environment. These companies were "more likely to invest in renewable power, to actively measure and reduce the environmental effects of their production and packaging, to implement carbon-reduction programs among their suppliers, to integrate the impact of climate change into their planning and financial decisions, to help customers manage climate change risks, to work actively to improve their operations' efficiency, and to minimize and mitigate biodiversity disturbances."[211]

209 Edwin Ng and Carles Muntaner, "The more women in government, the healthier a population," *The Conversation*, January 9, 2019.

210 Ibid.

211 Scott, *The Double X,* 26.

This led author Linda Scott, in her book *The Double X Economy: The Epic Potential of Women's Empowerment*, to conclude:

> Having been excluded from the world of high finance and quick riches throughout history, women appear to assess risk more realistically than do men. Having been charged with the cultivation of children, they seem to have a longer horizon than their male compatriots for return on investment, as well as greater aversion to long-term damage, such as is happening to the environment. Perhaps because of their historical emphasis on home and connection, women are more likely to invest in their communities, to give to charity, and to demand social responsibility from both the products and the stocks they buy.[212]

The argument Scott's book makes, in which I whole-heartedly agree, is for the first time in history we have a "vivid blueprint for eliminating suffering, achieving justice, and ensuring peace."[213] It's right here in front of our masked faces. Women in leadership matters. Women in leadership changes the world for the better. Women in leadership is the cure for what ails us.

GOT IT. SO, WHY IS THIS SO HARD?

While we're fortunate to live in an age with more and more women running, too often they continue to be presented with a series of broken rungs on the ladder to leadership: judgments for their appearances, their

212 Ibid.
213 Ibid, 27.

"likability," their comparable lack of experience, and lack of funding to stay in the game.

Writer Jessica Valenti summed this phenomenon up in her August 2020 article titled, "The VP Candidate Isn't Being Vetted. She's Being Scrutinized." The piece was written when US Presidential candidate Joe Biden was narrowing his choices of female running-mates. Valenti writes, "Kamala Harris is too ambitious; Elizabeth Warren is too much of a know-it-all; Stacey Abrams doesn't have enough experience. This is more than standard vetting—it's a live demonstration of the impossibly high standard women are held to, even when they're up for the *second*-most important job."[214]

The reality is, our deeply ingrained gender bias, whether conscious or unconscious, is standing in our way. Only 52 percent of Americans (45 percent of men and 60 percent of women) say they would feel "very comfortable" having a female president. Globally, the Reykjavik Index for Leadership ranks the G7 countries on the percentage of people who would be comfortable with a female head of state. The UK comes in at 58 percent, Canada 57 percent, Italy 42 percent, France 40 percent, Germany 25 percent, and Japan 23 percent.[215] Note that Germany *has* a female head of state and has for thirteen years, and the majority of people surveyed still can't get comfortable with the idea.

---

214 Jessica Valenti, "The VP Candidate Isn't Being Vetted. She's Being Scrutinized," *Medium,* August 4, 2020.

215 Zachary Basu, "52 percent of Americans would feel 'very comfortable' with a female president," *Axios,* November 27, 2018.

Our bias is aided by news coverage and social media, with a 2019 report finding that female candidates are "attacked significantly more than male candidates." The study also found the narratives on social media around female candidates were "more negative and focused on issues of character and identity, rather than electability or policy." As if that's not enough, the study also found female candidates receive more attacks from trolls and fake-news accounts and less coverage by traditional news media compared to their male counterparts.[216]

All of this leads to what the study ultimately coined a "gender penalty" for female candidates. This gender-penalty likely played a significant role in ensuring none of the five women originally running for the 2020 democratic nomination would make it very far. And while I'm grateful the 2020 election includes a woman for a VP candidate, it's frustrating to see a smart, capable woman once again be considered only second-best in line for the job.

THE MATRIARCHY

At an event in December of 2019, former President Barack Obama remarked, "I'm absolutely confident that for two years if every nation on earth was run by women, you would see a significant improvement across the board on just about everything... living standards and outcomes."[217] Having worked in the predominantly female non-profit industry my entire career, my own qualitative research aligned with this sentiment. But

216 Suyin Haynes, "Female 2020 Democratic Presidential Candidates Face a 'Gender Penalty' Online, Study Finds," *Time*, November 5, 2019.

217 Ebony Bowden, "Barack Obama says world would be a better place if run by women," *New York Post*, December 16, 2019.

now, having seen the quantitative data, I genuinely believe this to be true and couldn't be more proud to advocate that we make the matriarchy by getting more women into leadership roles.

We are our own worst enemies on progress in this corner. We have to acknowledge and change our gender lenses on leadership and remember the data—women in leadership are proven to be a very good thing. So, even if our wardrobe choices, or stray hairs and gray hairs, or "shrill" tones of voice are something we're not accustomed to seeing and hearing in leadership, we have to get comfortable with the uncomfortable and focus on the data and the facts.

A final puzzle piece I enjoyed greatly in this section is Tomas Chamorro-Premuzic's 2019 TED Talk titled, "Why Do So Many Incompetent Men Become Leaders?" In the talk, he argues while women face many barriers to leadership, we don't put up nearly *enough* barriers for the incompetent men in leadership roles. Chamorro-Premuzic roots his argument in the idea that when selecting leaders, we have a hard time discerning between confidence and competence and that charisma and charm are mistaken for leadership potential.

Studies show arrogance and overconfidence are inversely related to leadership talent. Instead, traits of successful leaders are high-levels of humility, emotional intelligence, and creative and flexible problem-solving. He finds it "odd" we ask women to "lean in" and adopt the over-confident traits we're accustomed to seeing from male leaders when there is compelling scientific evidence that women, who are found to be more sensitive, considerate, and humble than men, are more likely to adopt effective leadership strategies.

Chamorro-Premuzic therefore concludes: "The result is a pathological system that rewards men for their incompetence while punishing women for their competence to everybody's detriment."[218]

To our detriment indeed. It's time to change our lenses on leadership and make the matriarchy that will save us all.

The vision: **Equal representation by women in leadership at the federal, state, and local levels, from the halls of government to the hallways of the office. A culture that values and lifts up the true leadership skills of emotional intelligence, hubris, and inclusivity.**

---

218 Tomas Chamorro-Premuzic, "Why Do So Many Incompetent Men Become Leaders?" *Harvard Business Review,* August 22, 2013.

PART THREE

MAKING SENSE
OF IT ALL

CHAPTER 13

Let's Talk About
Those Nordics

In keeping with the puzzle analogy, we're at the point
where we identified the corners and locked into place
many adjoining pieces, but now we must scour for those
common thread pieces that pull the whole thing together.
On this journey, the common thread was the Nordics.

In each corner as I researched for places with concrete
evidence of progress, the Nordic region *kept coming up*. Of
the five countries included in the Nordic region (Denmark,
Iceland, Finland, Norway, and Sweden), four have female
prime ministers, their highest-ranking elected official.
They are consistently some of the highest-ranking countries on the Women, Peace and Security Index, with the
crown jewel, Iceland, ranking in the top 20 percent of each
of the eleven indicators of progress, the only country in
the world to do so. In the World Economic Forum Global
Gender Gap Index 2020, Iceland, Norway, Finland, and Sweden rank one to four for smallest gender gaps globally.[219]
And for anyone who follows the annual World Happiness

219 Global Gender Gap Report 2020.

Report, you'll find the Nordic countries have all been in the top ten every year since they started measuring in 2013.[220] While they still have room to grow (as, arguably, everyone always does), the Nordic region seems to be furthest along in building an inclusive and equitable society where residents are happier and healthier.

So, what can we learn from them?

"CAN AMERICAN MEN AND WOMEN EVER REALLY BE EQUAL?"

That title of Irin Carmon's 2018 *Time Magazine* article caught my eye, as it was the same question I had asked myself many times, both before and increasingly during this writing journey. Carmon sought out the answer by traveling to Stockholm to explore the place where in 2014 the country's prime minister, Stefan Löfven, had declared Sweden "the first feminist government in the world."[221] Carmon's goal was to spend time with the Swedes to see how that declaration was playing out in everyday life and what, if anything, the US could learn.

Carmon's article covers a vast array of what we can learn, both now, and throughout history. She points out the US has turned to Sweden for clues on governance as far back as the 1930s when President Franklin D. Roosevelt sent researchers to study how the country successfully forged a path between American capitalism and Soviet communism, results of which can been seen in the social

---

220 Frank Martela et. al., "The Nordic Exceptionalism: What Explains Why the Nordic Countries Are Constantly Among the Happiest in the World," *World Happiness Report*, March 20, 2020.

221 Irin Carmon, "Can American Men and Women Ever Really Be Equal?" *Time*, September 27, 2020.

The Power and Promise of Prioritizing Women

safety nets of the New Deal. But the US stopped short of doubling down on inclusive policies as Sweden would go on to do, which plays out in the global rankings on equality we see today.

In 1947, Sweden implemented a child allowance (a subsidy for expenses related to providing for children) and nationwide paid maternity leave by 1955. Policies continued to grow and evolve in the '70s when Sweden realized jointly taxing couples meant women worked less, so they started taxing individuals. In 1974, they became the first country in the world to offer paid paternity leave when they realized allowing only mothers to take leave meant women took on the lion share of household labor in the critical early months of establishing new routines as parents, and that set the stage for women taking on more for years to follow. Fast forward to today, Swedes enjoy all of the above, plus a monthly stipend of $142 per child and 480 days per child of shared parental leave (i.e., either parent can take it) up until the child turns eight.

As Carmon would witness firsthand during her time in Sweden, what emerges from more than seventy years of intentionally investing in gender equality is a more balanced society for everyone. Sweden and its Nordic neighbors have figured out how to be societies where there is a higher proportion of women in the workforce; a national curriculum educating future generations on gender equality; guaranteed paid parental leave; access to affordable childcare and a monthly allowance to cover childcare needs for all parents; and, as a result, a significantly narrowed gap between men and women when it comes to overall progress and prosperity.

Carmon's findings mirror those of author Anu Partanen whose book, *The Nordic Theory of Everything: In Search of a Better Life*, covers a wide-range of ways in which Nordic social constructs both benefit the entire society and have a positive effect on closing gender gaps.

Partanen wrote her book after growing up in Finland and eventually immigrating to the US to experience what she expected to be "the world's shining beacon of freedom, independence, individualism, and opportunity."[222] As she worked to settle in to her new life in the US, she found herself with a mounting and unfamiliar anxiety navigating health care, taxes, and employment. As she sets up in the book's prologue, she would discover "to leave Finland or any other Nordic country behind and settle in America at the beginning of the twenty-first century was to experience an extraordinary—and extraordinarily harsh—form of travel backward in time."[223]

Partanen's book is an eye-opening first-person experience of what it's like to live as a citizen in these two very different social constructs. While it's not written as a book on gender equality, the topic comes up frequently as an important outcome of inclusive social policies. She writes of "the Nordic theory of love," defined as a society in which "all individuals be self-sufficient, so that they can give more purely and generously of their affection and care."[224]

She translates this theory of love to point out that while the US purports to be about freedom and equality and

222 Anu Partanen, *The Nordic Theory of Everything: In Search of a Better Life*, (New York: Harper Paperbacks, 2017).

223 Ibid, 9.

224 Ibid, 93.

would never count itself among developing nations where women are dependent on men to live, the US social systems actually create a great amount of dependency. Partanen was raised with equal access to health care, paid parental leave, quality childcare, higher education, and retirement care because her country invested in her ability to prosper as a fully independent citizen. Instead, in the US, she found herself dependent on her marriage and her employer (if she could find one) to stay healthy and housed.

Partanen cited this dependency and others as the source of her newfound anxiety and stress. In Finland, stability and prosperity aren't linked to one's ability to marry and enjoy a dual-income household or get hired by the employer with the most generous benefits. This, in turn, takes a whole element of stress out of these relationships. As she writes, "Spouses avoid the dependencies and resentments that arise when one person pursues a career and controls the money, and the other person manages all the housework and the children."[225] Citizens as *individuals* are stronger both financially and emotionally, leading to happier and healthier parents, children, employees, and employers.

It struck me that while Partanen may have set out seeking a vision of a uniquely free and prosperous American experience, instead she experienced something else uniquely American: stress. Gallup's 2019 Global Emotions Report surveyed 151,000 adults from more than 140 countries to measure feelings and emotions about life. Fifty-five percent of respondents in the US reported feelings

---

225 Ibid, 93.

of high stress, while 45 percent reported feeling worried "a lot of the day."[226] These numbers are significantly higher than the global average of 35 percent, leaving the US tied for fourth with Albania, Iran, and Sri Lanka in Gallup's list of world's most stressed populations.[227] Women are more likely than men to report having a great deal of stress, and almost half of women report their stress levels have increased in recent years.[228]

Partanen was so struck by how awful she felt after moving to the US she decided to write a whole book about it. Her comparison left me wondering if Americans have settled for living with constant survival stress in ways the Nordic countries have deemed unacceptable in the modern day.

WHY WOMEN HAVE BETTER SEX UNDER SOCIALISM

By now, you may be wondering if this matriarchy I want to make is just socialism. Some (if they have read this far) may think I'm a *damn socialist*, or a *crazy liberal*, or (my favorite) *brainwashed*.

In the same way I struggle to find my place in the quest to "smash the patriarchy," I also struggle to sit comfortably with any labels about which political systems I'm for or against. I've striven to make this book apolitical, because it seems, in this day and age, as soon as you "are"

226 Gallup, "Gallup 2019 Global Emotions Report," accessed October 4, 2020.

227 Meilan Solly, "Americans Are Among the Most Stressed-Out People in the World, Reporting Negative Emotions at Highest Rates in a Decade," *Smithsonian Magazine*, Apr 26, 2019.

228 American Psychological Association, "Gender and Stress," News release, (last modified 2012).

whatever label, there's no margin for error in what you must believe. This has led us to an extremely polarized society, which is distracting us from the everyday misery most of us are tolerating.

Why Women Have Better Sex Under Socialism is, by far, my favorite title of anything I read on this learning journey. I wasn't quite sure what to expect when I ordered this book (admittedly after a few glasses of wine). I suppose I expected another book confirming how wonderful life is in the democratically social Nordic region. Instead, author Kristen R. Ghodsee would give me a tremendous lesson in socialist history.

Ghodsee is a professor of Russian and East European studies at the University of Pennsylvania and has spent her career studying what happens when countries transition from state socialism to capitalism. She's lived and studied in both eastern and western Germany and Bulgaria and has traveled frequently across her twenty-year career to gather first-hand experiences in places like Yugoslavia, Romania, Hungary, Bucharest, Budapest, and Warsaw.

While I had grown up being properly indoctrinated to understand life in all of these countries was just plan horrible, imagine my surprise to read Ghodsee had witnessed, both in person when living in these countries and years later in response to her writing about them, that "women were more likely than men to express a longing for the state socialist past because of the many tangible benefits women lost with the coming of democracy and capitalism."[229]

---

229 Ghodsee, *Why Women Have*, xv.

It is true generous social safety nets like childcare and paid maternity leave were created to support evil intentions: forcing all citizens to work for the sake of domestic outputs, higher birthrates, and world-domination. However, I had never stopped to consider through a different lens these were systems made possible for everyone, men and women equally, to have the support they needed to work and have their basic needs met (yes, so they could be forced to keep having babies and going to work.)

The Nordics realized this. As the Cold War wound down, while places like Russia, Hungary, and Poland dismantled their social safety nets in pursuit of free-markets, Denmark, Sweden, and Finland doubled down on combining the social safety nets of state-socialism with the freedoms of democracy. When described this way it's easy to see how today, in the Nordic region, women and men have the supports they need to work and live *and* have plenty of freedom to choose how they want to use those supports.

I share all of this to say I'm not exactly sure I fit neatly into any of the labels. I certainly don't want to *be labeled* and be written off for all of the connotations that come along with that label. What I am is intrigued. Intrigued when Ghodsee pointed out it was, in fact, the Soviet Union who put the first woman in space, Valentina Tereshkova, in 1963.[230] And also when she pointed out the world's first female foreign minister was Romanian Ana Pauker, who took office in December of 1947.[231] And intrigued by the long-term effects of socialist systems that put women in

---

230 Ibid, xiv.

231 Ibid, 100.

the workplace: as of 2019 the countries where the majority of scientists and engineers are women are Lithuania, Bulgaria, and Latvia.[232]

Were these governments perfect? Far from it. But it's hard to deny there were elements of their infrastructure aimed to include *all* of their citizens fully, regardless of gender, that had lasting effects for women we see evidence of today.

And, for the record, very little of Ghodsee's book is about sex. (There's nothing like the power of a clever title to lure readers in and teach them a few things.) But true to the title, she does cover the topic and the wide-range of studies measuring sexual satisfaction under various forms of government in East and West Germany, the later unified Germany, Czechoslovakia, Poland, Bulgaria, and, eventually, the US. Over and over, the studies found that when systems were in place to increase economic independence for women and better divide household labor, both men and women reported more and higher quality sex in their relationships. As Ghodsee argues, contemporary relationships "are formed within a social context infused with economistic thinking and saturated with stress." Remove those pressures and we are free "to have loving relationships based more on mutual affection than on material exchange."[233]

SO DO WE COPY AND PASTE NORDIC POLICY?

As Carmon would write in *Time* about Sweden specifically, it's true the country "hasn't yet achieved full

---

232 Sandrine Amiel, "Women in Science: Five countries that beat the gender gap," *Euronews*, last modified November 2, 2019.

233 Ghodsee, *Why Women Have,* 150.

equality."[234] In all of the Nordic countries, women are still paid less than men, are still underrepresented in leadership and boardrooms, and have not-to-be-ignored statistics around sexual violence. But, for the most part, their statistics are lower than the rest of the world on each of these measures, which is why they rank so highly overall on global measurement tools. So, no, gender equality can't be checked off of the to-do list in the Nordic region either, but it's hard to deny the installation of strong social policies for the masses have a net positive impact on the lives of women.

Spending time examining the Nordic region allowed me to wrestle with my understanding of freedom. *Merriam-Webster* defines freedom as "the quality or state of being free: such as the absence of necessity, coercion, or constraint in choice or action."[235] Common school of thought in the US is things like state-sponsored health care, universal childcare, and free education are evidence of government overstepping; that by government providing these things, they are *constraining choices,* or *coercing families* to live their lives a certain way. Freedom is promoted as freedom of choice.

Partanen argues, however, nations that are truly progressing in the twenty-first century view freedom as "the assurance that all individuals get real opportunity, so they're free to pursue the good life for themselves, and real protection from the lottery of bad luck, so they're free from unnecessary fear and anxiety."[236] Essentially,

234 Carmon, "Can American Men."

235 *Merriam-Webster,* s.v. "Freedom," accessed October 6, 2020.

236 Partanen, *The Nordic Theory,* 325.

Partanen argues a government who provides true freedom of choice in the modern world creates a level playing field for all by providing the basic things people need to survive and thrive. This means each citizen is fully free from birth to make their own choices, regardless of their family wealth or abilities. And, even if you falter in your choices, there's no fear of complete loss of necessities on the other side. This, to me, is *true* freedom.

Running a company has further solidified this concept for me. For my employees, I am their source of basic needs that make for a healthy and prosperous life: health insurance, retirements savings, and parental leave benefits directly, and indirectly, the income they need to squirrel away for college educations, insurance co-pays, or whatever unexpected disaster might come along on top of that. That's a tremendous weight of dependency lurking around the office daily that can make it hard to separate people from performance. And, knowing what I now know about the economic barriers women face, the stakes feel all that much higher in my predominantly female workforce.

It's freeing to think of running a company where we can measure each other openly and honestly on performance and job satisfaction without the fear of utter loss looming in the room when things aren't going well. True freedom is knowing your necessities will come, no matter what, from birth to death, from a place that can't terminate you without cause. How might you lead your life differently with that kind of freedom?

In the making of the matriarchy, we must be open to exploring systems old and new and using these highly developed human brains we've inherited to evaluate and pursue new freedoms. The Nordic region offers some tremendous clues. It's time to understand and emulate the best of Nordic social policies and debunk the stereotypes so many Western societies are quick to apply: that they are a "socialist nanny-state," or irrelevant because the countries are smaller and more homogeneous, or taxes are far greater than in the US (they are slightly higher, but by the time you add up the return on investment of childcare, healthcare, higher education, paid leave, and retirement benefits, they start to look like a bargain).

The takeaway lesson here is while the Nordics certainly haven't achieved perfection, they are striving for it and redefining success, as necessary. And, while the Nordic countries jostle each year for top rankings in gender equality indexes, the US and other developed countries stubbornly ignore or radicalize the important social policies helping them get there and fall farther and farther behind.

It's becoming clear we are our own worst enemies if we simply write off particular social systems based on what we *think* we know about them. Rather, we must accept the current systems have evolved to a point where they are working for very few of us and perhaps the most patriotic thing we can do is educate ourselves about where in the world things are going well, why they are going well, and how we can draw from those examples to build a new society we are proud to be a part of.

CHAPTER 14:

Backsliding:
A Cautionary Tale

——

Speaking of falling behind, while hungrily exploring the best places in the world to be a woman, I realized I had largely overlooked the worst places to be a woman. To be fair, I did set out to figure out how to make the dream society of the future, not to wane on about where it sucks most to be a woman. But my research started to reveal a fatal flaw in this thinking, because some of the worst places in the world to be a woman hadn't always been that way.

On all of the gender indexes I had explored, there were just as many places falling behind in the rankings as there were advancing. It was a reminder that achieving equality isn't a finite venture. Advances can be lost far quicker and easier than they are won, especially when there are sexist people actively working against progress. It's irresponsible to talk about progress without also talking about preservation. In fact, preservation may be some of the most important work we can all commit to.

THE PROGRESS LINE GRAPH

Previous to this journey, if you had asked me to draw a line graph representing historical progress on women's rights in the US, I would have drawn a line of increases and plateaus. This being a reflection of what little women's history my education exposed me to, focusing on the periods of gains with little discourse on what happened in between.

On this journey I would come to know the periods of gains were known as the "waves of feminism," the three or four (the jury is still out on which wave we're in now) periods of time in the US in which there were large, well-organized movements that resulted in significant gains in rights for women.

The first wave is defined as the period from 1848 to 1920 in which suffragettes lobbied for many rights, with their biggest achievement being the nineteenth amendment granting women the right to vote. The second wave is defined as the period of time from 1963 to the 1980s that focused more on political and social equity and resulted in the Equal Pay Act of 1963, the creation of Title IX calling for educational equality, and 1973's *Roe v. Wade* codifying women's reproductive freedom. Within this wave also came the ability for women to apply for credit cards and mortgages under their own names, greater awareness and protection for domestic and sexual violence, and prevention of sexual harassment in the workplace.[237]

The third and maybe fourth waves are defined as beginning in 1991 and potentially continuing all the way through

237 Constance Grady, "The waves of feminism, and why people keep fighting over them, explained," *Vox*, July 20, 2018.

to present day. The wave begins with Anita Hill testifying before the Senate Judiciary Committee that Supreme Court Justice nominee Clarence Thomas had sexually harassed her at work, followed by what would be dubbed "the Year of the Woman" in 1992 when twenty-four women won seats in the House of Representatives and three won seats in the Senate. This wave advocated for more rights in the workplace and more women in leadership, but it is without similar landmark legislation of the first two waves. Those who argue we're currently in a fourth wave point to the #MeToo and Time's Up movements, the Women's Marches on Washington, and the record number of women running for and elected to office.[238]

I share these waves of feminism because I believe they are how I had constructed my progress line graph to be a series of peaks connected by plateaus. Without any knowledge of what happens in between peaks, it's easy to assume they are mostly periods of enjoying newly won rights. But rather, as digging into the data was showing me, it may very well be the true line graph of progress is a series of peaks, followed by plateaus, followed by gradual declines. And it's this episodic erosion that ultimately fuels the next peak.

When you peek between the peaks, you find sneaky sexist maneuvers. Like how after Arabella Mansfield became the first woman lawyer in 1869, in 1873 the Supreme Court would rule states had the right to exclude married women from practicing law.[239] Or how the Equal Rights Amendment (ERA), originally drafted in 1923 to codify

---

238 Ibid.

239 Susan Milligan, "Stepping Through History," *US News,* January 20, 2017.

equal rights for men and women in the US Constitution, was proposed to congress every year between 1923 and 1970 and only ever made it to the floor for a vote in 1946 where it failed. Later, when the ERA neared a deadline to ratify by 1979 that was later extended to 1982, a well-coordinated "STOP ERA" campaign was successfully waged, leaving us with the ERA yet to pass today.[240]

Deliberate efforts to set back progress for women are hidden in plain sight practically everywhere. The Comprehensive Child Development Act of 1971 would have established a national public childcare program in the US, universally available to all families and destined to make women's participation in the workforce easier. The bipartisan bill passed in both the House and the Senate and was widely viewed as a sensible investment in children and families. Upon arriving on President Nixon's desk, however, Nixon vetoed the bill, pandering to supporters who viewed the bill as overstepping into the private lives and choices of families.[241]

And while that missed opportunity may seem like unfortunate ancient history, progress is being challenged right under our noses in the present day. Most newsworthy, of course, are the sweeping efforts to roll back women's health protections secured in *Roe v. Wade*, but getting less attention are systemic setbacks on things like equal pay.

Equal pay has been a legislative topic dating all the way back to 1870, with various bills proposed throughout history to protect and promote equal pay for all. In

240 Meagan Day, "The story of the Equal Rights Amendment and the woman who killed it," *Medium,* September 7, 2016.

241 Anna Halperin, "Richard Nixon bears responsibility for the pandemic's child-care crisis," *Washington Post,* August 6, 2020.

2016, rules were enacted to support the enforcement of fair pay legislation, which was often one of the biggest challenges. The rules required companies with more than one hundred employees to submit their data on wages and demographics, including gender, to the Equal Employment Opportunity Commission each year so the gaps could be accurately recorded and addressed. These rules were set to go into effect in 2017 but were reversed by the new administration, cited as "too burdensome" for companies.[242]

You may recall in our examination of economic empowerment, Iceland recognized that effects of equal pay legislation were limited as long as the burden of proof was on employees.[243] Like the US, Iceland has had fair pay laws on the books since the 1960s, but a stubborn pay gap persisted. So, in 2018 they became the first in the world to pass a mandatory equal pay certification law requiring companies with twenty-five employees or more to certify they are paying men and women equally.[244] In 2016, the US could have pushed us one step closer to the bold action Iceland took, requiring companies to bear the burden of proof on gender pay gaps. But, with one pen stroke, progress evaporated, likely without many of us noticing.

Digging into history showed me the line graph is not always on the incline. While it has certainly inclined more than declined over time, there are stories of small

242 Danielle Zoellner, "Five major things Trump has done to roll back women's rights," *Independent,* March 6, 2020.

243 Camila Domonoske, "Companies in Iceland Now Required to Demonstrate They Pay Men, Women Fairly," *NPR,* January 3, 2018.

244 Government of Iceland, "Equal Pay Certification," accessed October 10, 2020.

declines buried within that limit greater progress over time. I wonder what life would be like today had the Comprehensive Child Development Act of 1971 passed. Would childcare feel less like a minefield of safety and affordability? Would an entire generation, raised through fair and equal access to care, be achieving better outcomes? Would the US rank higher on the gender equality indexes? What are these small declines costing us over time?

The truth is, while we have achieved a lot leading up to this point, there is both a tremendous amount of room for growth and a tremendous threat to losing progress that has been made.

THE CAUTIONARY TALE

Iran is a lesson in how a political revolution can erase progress quickly and with lasting effect.

During what was called the Pahlavi era from 1925 to 1979, Iran was on track with the rest of the world in making advances for women and families. Iran's first university, Tehran University, admitted both men and women when it opened in 1936. Women gained the right to vote and run for parliament in 1963. By 1978, twenty-two women sat in parliament, 333 women served on elected local councils, one-third of university students were female, and two million women were in the workforce.[245]

The 1979 Islamic Revolution politicized the lives of Iranian women, systematically reducing women's presence in the workforce from 13 percent to 8.6 percent; kicking women out of government and barring them from

245 Haleh Esfandiari, "The Women's Movement," *The Iran Primer*, October 6, 2010.

political positions; closing government-run daycare centers, forcing women into traditional childcare roles; mandating dress and head cover; and reducing the age of legal marriage from eighteen to nine.[246]

I found a photo essay on Iranian women pre- and post-revolution. The dates on the photos ranged from 1971 to 2008 and demonstrated how radically and enduringly the 1979 Revolution set back progress and freedoms for women.

The photos from the early 1970s look much like the photos in my mother's and grandmother's memory books. Some black and white, some in grainy color, they feature women with long flowing hairstyles, wide-collared shirts with funky prints, and bell-bottomed women and men seen together enjoying picnics in the park or posing in front of large boxy cars.[247]

But then, in 1979, a dramatic shift occurred. A photo of a group of female protesters taken in March of 1979 again looks recognizable: hair down, big barrettes, and chunky sweaters. And yet photos from later in the year show women with head-scarves and chadors—the cloak that covers the body from head to toe and leaves only the face exposed. Women and men do appear together in some photos, but separated and more conscious of keeping personal space between genders. As the years evolve, restrictions relax, and colors come back into attire while headscarves remain. The essay ends, however, with a 2005 photo of a family at the beach, with three women

246 Ibid.

247 n.a. "Iranian women—before and after the Islamic Revolution," *BBC*, February 8, 2019.

in headscarves and rolled-up pants wading in the water while a man in a speedo lays on the sand.[248] This final photo is a stark reminder of the lasting effects of gender inequality since the revolution.

While a political revolution with such dramatic outcomes may feel impossible in the US, it's important to note these laws didn't all change in a day. Laws in the US aren't changing overnight either, nor are the rules they govern as dramatic and restrictive as they were in Iran in the '70s and '80s. But US laws are changing with a focus on restricting women specifically, which ties directly to the politics of present day. Perhaps a cautionary tale in the making.

In May of 2019, Alabama legislators passed the most restrictive anti-abortion law in the country, banning abortion for all but very limited reasons. Rape and incest aren't included, and the legislation calls for doctors who perform abortions to be treated as felons and face up to ninety-nine years in prison. In the same month, Louisiana passed the "heartbeat bill" with no exceptions for rape or incest. Other states altering their abortion laws to be more restrictive in 2019 included Mississippi, Ohio, Georgia, Missouri, Kentucky, Arkansas, Utah, and Iowa. Further, states working to pass anti-abortion bills included South Carolina, West Virginia, Florida, and Texas.[249]

As I have advocated this entire journey, I believe it is important to look around the world and draw parallels we can learn from. Political upheaval dramatically impacted the lives of women in Iran, but not overnight.

---

248 Ibid.

249 Alexandra Hutzler, "These Are All The States That Have Passed Anti-Abortion Laws in 2019," *Newsweek*, May 31, 2019.

Rather, as the number of conservative leaders grew, so did the number of rules that collectively compounded restrictions for women.

Through this lens it's important to see the surge in legislation designed to challenge women's rights across the US comes on the heels of a political appointment. On October 6, 2018, President Donald Trump appointed Justice Brett Kavanuagh to the US Supreme Court. Kavanuagh had a long history as a conservative judge, including on issues around abortion. With Kavanaugh's appointment, the predominant political ideology of the court swung conservative, creating what legislators in Alabama and Louisiana saw as a window of opportunity to overturn the rights women had won in 1973's *Roe v. Wade* ruling.

Hopefully, you're beginning to see how the pieces of regression come together and recognize Iran for the cautionary tale it is. No matter your views on the topic of abortion, these are legislative efforts to undo previously-won rights of women. Period. If these laws are overturned, it preserves the ideology that it's acceptable to pass legislation that impacts only women, creating opportunity to reconsider reversing other hard-won rights as well. This would be unfortunate for women in the US, no doubt, but we must also consider when a world leader like the United States behaves in this way, it sends a clear message to the rest of the world that limiting the freedoms of women is still acceptable.

DISSENT TO DELUSIONS OF GRANDEUR

The biggest barrier to achieving equality in the US may be our willingness to believe we are the best and all we have achieved will never go away. It's easy to look around at the diversity of women living and working freely and conclude anything is possible with hard work. With this conclusion, we dangerously ignore or endure the oppression and inequality looming in our lives and chalk it up to just being part of the journey, convincing ourselves that even in the best places to live everything can't be perfect, right?

Ambivalence leads to inaction. Inaction leads to a static state. Standing still while others move forward means you get left behind. And the US is very much falling behind. Consider:

- Between 2018 and 2020, the United States dropped two places to number fifty-three in Global Gender Gap Index produced by the World Economic Forum. The US's overall score has only increased by 0.020 points since 2006 (by contrast, Iceland, ranked at number one in both 2018 and 2020, has gained 0.095 points since 2006, and next best Norway has gained 0.043 since 2006).[250]

- The US joins Papua New Guinea as the only two countries in the world without legally guaranteed paid maternity leave.[251]

- The US joins Iran, Palau, Somalia, Sudan, and Tonga as the only six UN countries who have not ratified the 1979 international women's bill of rights, formally called the Convention on the Elimination of All Forms of Discrimination Against Women (CEDAW).[252]

250 Global Gender Gap Report 2020.

251 GIWPS, *Women, Peace, and Security Index 2017/2018,* accessed October 10, 2020.

252 Scott, *The Double X,* 284.

- In the 2018 Global Peace and Security Index, the US ranked sixty-sixth in the security rankings because rates of intimate partner violence were 10 percentage points above the mean for developed countries. Similarly, 46 percent of men report feeling safe walking alone at night in the US, while only 26 percent of women do. This 20-percentage point gap is more than twice the average gap of seven points.[253]

- According to Save the Children, the US ranks thirty-third on the Mothers' Index, which assess the well-being of mothers and children in 179 countries.[254]

Now, I'm not here to argue that the US needs to be number one. Rather, I'm here to argue that until we are, we need to stop ignoring that we aren't.

We are not the best. We are not the best. We are not the best. We need to get that through our heads. *We are not.* Yes, we are not the worst. But we are quickly falling behind on what a society needs to thrive in the modern day. And if we continue to ignore the issues pulling us down, I think we can expect our children and grandchildren to seriously consider immigrating to countries who are investing in gender equality and more inclusive societies.

For anyone inclined to say, "Fine, go, good riddance," to those youthful expats, I invite them to view this from a brain-drain perspective. Brain-drain is defined as "the departure of educated or professional people from one country, economic sector, or field, usually for better pay

---

253 GIWPS, *Index 2017/2018.*

254 Save the Children, "The Urban Disadvantage 2015 Report," accessed October 10, 2020.

or living conditions."[255] With women predominantly filling the halls of higher education, what if those future doctors, nurses, professors, engineers, and scientists decide to depart to countries that demonstrate greater protection of their rights and value of their presence? Imagine the potential ripple effect across society.

The truth is while we have achieved a lot leading up to this point, there is both a tremendous amount of room for growth and a tremendous threat to losing progress that has been made. When it comes to picking our pieces of the gender equality puzzle to focus on, working on preservation is just as important as working on progress. Much like a real puzzle, if some nefarious person started plucking pieces out of the sections you've already completed, you would recognize this setback and swat their sticky hands away from your masterpiece. It is the same in this work. We must protect the pieces we've assembled as part of the journey to whole, lest we wind up a cautionary tale.

---

255 *Merriam-Webster*, s.v. "Brain Drain," accessed October 10, 2020.

CHAPTER 15:

From Puzzle, to Personal, to Pandemic

"Fight for the things you care about, but do it in a way that will lead others to join you."

—JUSTICE RUTH BADER GINSBURG

I had reached the point in my writing and research journey where it was time to start wrapping up. Deadlines were approaching, and it was not lost on me I could keep writing on this ever-evolving subject and never actually publish.

Where I had hoped months of researching and connecting with experts would give me a clear to-do list on what it will take to achieve gender equality in my lifetime, what I had compiled so far was looking more like a giant, multi-layered wall of sticky notes. I wondered if I had talked to the right people, asked the right questions, or if I was ready to publish at all.

One day, while reviewing a list of additional experts I was hoping to interview before deadline, it hit me: I could probably talk to a thousand more experts and still not reveal the "big goal" I felt I was searching for. It struck me that my puzzle analogy was right all along. There are pieces to the gender equality puzzle all around us, and the true "big goal" is to get educated about what matters to each of us and devote a part of our lives to making those pieces click into the larger work.

Or, as Rebecca Roberts, co-author of *The Suffragist Playbook: Your Guide to Changing the World*, would tell me in one of my final interviews: "Find something that lights your fire."

I first heard Rebecca speak at a fundraising event for the suffragist memorial in development to join the monuments and memorials in Washington, DC. She shared the sentiment that at the time suffragists were pursuing votes for women it was considered as radical as if I were to advocate for giving cats the right to vote today. But the suffragists doggedly pursued and persevered for more than seventy-two years, made the radical seem less radical, and changed culture along the way.

When I asked Rebecca her advice for people looking to make progress, she said she shies away from the idea that women should do a certain thing. "Everybody gets to make the decision for themselves on where and how they are going to get involved," she said. "The only wrong choice is not doing anything."

I shared my puzzle analogy with Rebecca and that I felt I was still soul-searching for a "big goal." She reminded me that focusing on one big goal can feel hopeless at times, and the last thing you want to feel as an activist is hopeless. Instead, she advised, we must celebrate the incremental victories and occasionally poke our heads up from each of our corners of the puzzle and see beyond our few pieces.

Like Rebecca, everyone I've talked to (and would still like to talk to!) are literal reflections of pieces of the puzzle; experts in gender policy, leadership, women's rights, health, and equality. They are people working globally, nationally, and locally with a wide-range of skills in communications, community organizing, policy, research, fundraising, leadership, parenting, and more. Each had passionate stories about why they do what they do and big dreams on what they hope they will help to achieve in their lifetimes.

MY PIECES

The third and fourth waves of feminism have been criticized for not having specific clear legislative goals like the first and second waves did. It leads to calling these waves into question for whether they are waves at all; whether the half million people who attended the 2017 Women's March on Washington represents a movement or a moment.

The answer is yes.

Yes, it was a feel-good moment, and momentous moments are what send us all home energized to make change and fuel a movement. Yes, there may not (yet) be a clear piece of legislation that defines this or future waves of feminism, but perhaps that is because instead of the peak-plateau-decline lines of progress of our past, modern day movements are about the steady incline; day by day knocking down oppression big and small, changing our language, behaviors, mindsets, textbooks, schools, workplaces, legislators, policies, structures, and, ultimately, culture.

This journey would reveal to me the fierce feminist in my core whose physical presence I had felt from a young age but didn't know how to describe until now. I felt her every weekend when my parents dragged me to Catholic mass, and I felt something burning in my core toward the grouchy old men on the alter invoking dominance and shame over me. I felt her in my early career days working for a law school, where at alumni gatherings older male alumni and administrators would send me off to fetch drinks, and I felt "frustrated" I wasn't further along in my career and earning more respect. She was there when my daughter received the "best smile" superlative at her kindergarten graduation, causing my body to tense and my brain to urge me to run on stage and tell her not to *ever* let anyone tell her the best thing about her is her smile. She's been in there all along, but I just chalked up all her nudging to other things.

Now that I know she's there, I feel like she's about to explode out of my chest. I feel her more now, when a husband makes a joke about his wife, when anyone tells a woman or girl she's overreacting, when men interrupt women at work, and so many more. She's there hollering at me about my own life, screaming, "You found me! Now get out there and channel me into your voice to empower other women! Use your energetic superpowers to lift women up and help them find their own superpowers! Stop putting the responsibilities of wife and mother first

The Power and Promise of Prioritizing Women

before all else and hiding behind the fear of total ruin if you put yourself out there and fail."

My fierce feminist is now armed with knowledge. The knowledge that empowering women and striving for gender equality *will* change the world for the better. She knows she's armed with privilege too. She's trained to see the pains of dependency baked into everyday life for women and to challenge any limiting beliefs previously accepted and seek alternatives that empower all. It's like the fierce feminist who has been living in my gut for so long now has a direct line to a better brain, and together they are ready to change the world.

Empowerment[256]

2. The state of being empowered to do something: the power, right, or authority to do something

My journey has left me feeling exactly what *Merriam-Webster* defines as empowerment: *in a state of being empowered to do something.* In executing this commitment I made to learn what it will take to build a more gender equal society in my lifetime, I have arrived at the end of this journey feeling eager, enraged, enlightened, exhausted, emboldened, and empowered. Mostly, empowered.

So, what do I do with all of this energy building up like electricity under my skin?

For starters, I'm going to commit my professional life to this work. Today, that means continuing to show up in my interim CEO role, serving both the survivors of violence and trauma we help and my predominantly female workforce. If I decide to apply for the full-time role, I'm

256 *Merriam-Webster,* s.v. "Empowerment," accessed September 26, 2020.

giving thought to what my gender equality initiatives would be during my leadership. Thanks to this journey, I'm confident I would work to double down on growing violence prevention education efforts in the community; partnering with advocacy organizations to fight for the important policy work that will eliminate the cycles of dependency keeping so many people in abusive relationships; re-examining internal compensation, hiring, and promotion structures to ensure greater equity across all races and abilities; and eliminating any of our "ideal worker" fueled policies and practices.

In truth, however, I'm weighing if (or perhaps when) I want to go bigger. While it would be a tremendous honor to stay at Doorways and serve my local community and our fifty-one-person team, it is not lost on me this role, work, and organization are just one small piece of the puzzle. And, arguably, it is a piece of the puzzle designed predominantly to respond life-altering injustice after it has happened, rather than creating the systemic change needed to prevent it in the first place.

This is where I find myself being called to "go bigger." Not in title, organization size, compensation, or service-area, but in impact. This journey has shown me the critical role policy and leadership play in enacting change. That while we can make micro-adjustments in our own lives, the proven pathway to big change is in the laws and policies that impact all of society and the leaders who model behavioral change that transforms culture.

Here, I can start with my vote. I can train myself to look beyond the headlines that will ask me to judge the quality of the candidate by their age, appearance, tone of voice, party, marital status, parental status, or other applied labels. Instead, I can take the time to explore their gen-der-policy platforms, or lack thereof, which is also telling. As the Nordic countries have demonstrated, working to achieve gender equality is a choice a country can actively take, so it's critical those we entrust to govern see this work just as much a part of their plan as transportation, health, education, and the other areas we expect to see. Expect more.

I'm going to change how I talk to my daughter about her body and her sexuality. I now recognize chastely tiptoe-ing around the topic because of cultural conditioning and relying on sex-ed classes at school is a complete failure in my role as a parent. If we want to change culture around sex and power, it's important we educate future gener-ations to think and act differently.

I will also listen carefully to my daughter about the lenses of possibility she's creating for herself. When math is too hard, I'll recall perhaps she isn't getting the same support and encouragement as her male classmates, and without it math *is* much harder. I'll check my own gender tendencies when it comes to parenting boys and girls, and help my friends do the same. We'll keep each other accountable for raising our kids in more gender-neutral ways.

I will change what I tolerate and what I expect in social circles. No longer will I nervously laugh along at sexist jokes or assume the women will do all the cooking and cleaning while the men relax and drink beer at gather-ings. The rules at my house will be different.

I will own the shit out of my educated white-lady priv-ilege. I will acknowledge that many forms of feminism and feminist policy serve predominantly white women, and those who are anything but straight white ladies like me may not benefit from what I think is good. I will seek to understand rights for *all* women and ensure I leverage my privilege to create pathways for all.

I will acknowledge and work to rectify the fact that my education was heavily influenced by gender stereotypes. My textbooks and curriculum were largely written and designed by men through their gender and political lenses. This has resulted in me not knowing nearly enough about all the amazing women who have been changing the world for centuries and not seeing nearly enough role models to decide how I would shape mine. I will stop assuming curriculum has been updated with the passage of time and work to ensure children are exposed to more. I will also recognize that my history text books trained me to see democracy and capitalism and perfect systems, whereas now I know there are a depth of insights we can gain from socialist and matriarchal structures and how some of their best qualities invest in women in ways that benefit all.

I will embrace my place in history as a tremendous advantage point and recognize I need to keep learning more about history to fully leverage that advantage. The majority of sources for this book were published in the last decade, many in the last few years. Gender equality is being studied more than ever before, which means we have the data to inform decision-making like never before. The opportunity to combine data and examples of societal structures that have come before us is a tremendous place of advantage from which to choose wisely in how we move forward.

I will keep using my voice to shape the collective conscience. Social media, being the blessing and curse that it is, is an incredibly easy place to routinely share the puzzle pieces I will continue to seek and collect as part of a life-long learning journey. Culture is created by collective regard, so I will work to ensure more of us regard gender equality as an essential element.

I'll also use social media for good to keep up with the amazing organizations working on the front lines of gender equality I learned of on this journey. I've started following Equality Can't Wait, Women Moving Millions, UN Women, Women Deliver, Equal Measures 2030, Global Fund for Women, and the National Women's Law Center. I'll keep searching and exploring for more.

As I'm nearing the end of this writing journey, I certainly don't know all of the solutions, but I know where I stand: ready to serve this critical and long-overdue mission of persistently pursuing gender equality.

THE CORONAVIRUS PANDEMIC: ESCALATOR OR ANCHOR?

I've touched on the impacts of the coronavirus pandemic at different points throughout the book. It's a hard thing to write about when we're still in the middle of it, and the impact is changing daily.

What will perhaps make this topic most evergreen for the sake of a book is to acknowledge the great pause the pandemic caused can either be seized as a tremendous opportunity to rebuild a society that serves to close the gender gap, or to rapidly erase decades of hard-won progress.

On a new section of their website, Women Deliver boldly claims, "A Gender Equal World is Healthier, Wealthier, and

Possible."[257] The page is a tremendous resource that aligns with much of what I have discovered and shared in this book, and it also stresses the importance of applying a gender lens to respond and recover from the COVID-19 pandemic.

As if they had previewed the four corners of my puzzle, the site highlights the additional challenges the pandemic is creating globally in women's health, domestic violence, women's employment, and education for girls. Specifically:[258]

- Disruptions in reproductive health services will lead to fifteen million unintended pregnancies, twenty-eight thousand maternal deaths, and 3.3 million unsafe abortions across 132 low- and middle-income countries over twelve months;

- Domestic violence cases will increase by fifteen million additional cases for every three months of continued restrictions and stay-at-home orders;

- Nearly 510 million women, representing 40 percent of female employment, are in jobs that have been negatively impacted by the pandemic, erasing hard-won gains in women's employment rates and threatening the economic stability of women and families;

- Approximately 743 million girls are out of school, the poorest of whom are at greater risk of early forced marriage or dropping out entirely to help with care giving needs.

In the US specifically, the 2020 Women in the Workplace report, published in September 2020, focuses almost

257 Generation Equality, "Women Deliver," accessed October 11, 2020.
258 Ibid.

exclusively on how COVID-19 has negatively impacted women in the workplace. It found women, especially women of color, are more likely to have been laid off or furloughed; are twice as likely as fathers to worry their performance is being judged negatively because of caregiving responsibilities; and one in four women are contemplating downshifting their careers or leaving the workforce entirely.[259]

And yet while 25 percent of women are considering quitting their jobs due to work-family conflict, so are an unprecedented 11 percent of men.[260] With many professionals working remotely, it's an opportunity to question the ideal worker expectations and for both parents to see first-hand how difficult balancing work and parenting expectations is.

The World Economic Forum has taken an opportunistic approach, advocating "as we stand in the middle of this historic inflection point, now is our moment to come together as a global community and close the gender gap once and for all—to establish a new, more inclusive world order; a new, more inclusive social contract."[261] They urge leaders to engage women in decision-making processes, to disaggregate economic data by gender to fully understand and budget for recovery, to use a gender

259 McKinsey & Company, "Women in the Workplace 2020," accessed October 11, 2020; Marianne Cooper, "Mothers' Careers Are at Extraordinary Risk Right Now," *The Atlantic*, October 1, 2020; McKinsey & Company, "Women," 6.

260 Joan C. Williams, "The Pandemic Has Exposed the Fallacy of the 'Ideal Worker,'" *Harvard Business Review*, May 11, 2020.

261 Katica Roy, "Here's how to achieve gender equality after the pandemic," *World Economic Forum*, April 25, 2020.

lens to craft relief programs, and to ensure impact by using gender-based assessments.

Escalator or anchor. We have choices. And, as the World Economic Forum also adds so poignantly, "we are rapidly exhausting our list of excuses when it comes to achieving gender equality."[262]

---

262 Ibid.

CHAPTER 16:

No More Gangster Baboons

Writing a book is hard. Writing a book in ten months is harder. Writing a book in ten months during a global pandemic during which you're serving as an interim CEO for an organization serving survivors of domestic violence and sexual assault and also runs two congregate setting shelters with little room for social distancing is the hardest. There were plenty of times I didn't think I would make it: when the words wouldn't flow; when the deadlines were too close; when the interviews got rescheduled; when the feedback was too hard to hear. But I believe in the power of the universe to push us in the directions we need to be pushed, and when it felt like I was limping toward the finish line on this writing journey I received a nudge forward.

It was day 215 of serving in the interim CEO role, but it was starting to feel more like day 2,015. The realities of 2020 were taking a hard tole on my teams. Practically overnight, we had figured out how to socially distance our service models where possible; how to procure PPE (personal protective equipment) and enforce staff and residents to wear it; how to move high-risk residents into hotels so they could socially distance but still provide the critical wrap-around services they need; and how to chase all the different pots of aid money flowing through our state and local governments so we could afford all these changes. And that was just at work. Outside of work, my majority-minority workforce was facing repeated reminders of racial injustice, all while socially isolated in quarantine, constantly reminded that working with others (which is what makes most of them thrive) could be a silent killer.

My harsh reality was people were quitting. Or, more importantly, women were quitting. I suspect it was a combination of residual turnover bound to happen with the departure of the previous CEO, simply delayed by the uncertainty of the job market in the early days of coronavirus. But now there were women quitting who, when I met them in February, seemed to have no intention of leaving and were rooting for me to stay in the position long-term. The only thing that had changed was *nearly everything had changed* in the lives of these women, and it was too much. For whatever their reasons, they were bailing out.

This left me, either hilariously or terrifyingly, serving as the direct supervisor to our counseling department. Me, who has no background in social work or counseling, let alone counseling for trauma. Heck, it was only in the last ten years of my life I had finally shaken off the shame I had been raised with around "people who go to counseling" and went to counseling myself. To say I was feeling more out of my depth than ever before was an understatement. So, when one of our counselors reached out to me for help navigating a client challenge, I took a nervous gulp and accepted the call.

The counselor would share she was working with a client whose recovery journey was at a crossroad. The client, let's call her Nina, was a mother with a nineteen-month-old child. Nina had bravely left her abusive partner, navigated seeking and securing shelter, establishing safety, and about four weeks earlier finding a job she was excited about because it was in her field of interior design. We had helped Nina get this far, subsidizing the private babysitter that cost $350 per week, because the $8 per hour she was being paid in training was barely enough to cover the rest of their living expenses. Her plan had been to transition into the more affordable early head-start childcare center at the end of her four-week training, which was the same time her pay would increase to $15 per hour. With that plan in place, income and childcare would begin to stabilize, and her journey to self-sufficiency could progress.

But things weren't going to plan for Nina. Her new employer was requiring an extra week of training, meaning one more week of barely scraping by financially. This came at the same time the head-start center, which had been closed since the spring because of COVID-19, announced they weren't going to make their target September reopening and now were "hoping" to be ready by October. The reason the counselor called me was because Nina was weighing whether she would need to quit her job to care for her child because she couldn't afford the $350 per week babysitter, and she didn't want to assume our organization would or could continue subsidizing her. Nina had run through her other options only to find more barriers: she had no friends or family in the area because she had relocated here with her husband in the lead; the child's father technically owed childcare, but she feared asking him outright would trigger more violence, and collecting it through the courts would take too long; and to add literal insult to injury, she had applied for a program that would subsidize childcare for the long-haul, but was denied because she fell $56 short of the income requirements.

As the counselor and I worked together to problem-solve, I realized the universe had shoved me closer to the work so I could remember that Nina could be any woman. She was an educated woman who had overcome tremendous challenges that included fearing for her life at the hands of her partner. Now, she was being forced to choose between pursuing a career that would lead her to self-sufficiency and stability, or quitting for lack of childcare, likely plunging her into cycles of poverty, instability, dependency, depression, and more.

Armed with my newfound knowledge, I could see with just one critical systematic difference, guaranteed access to affordable childcare, this brave woman wouldn't be at this life-altering fork in the road. While I had never met Nina, and likely never would, I felt incredibly close to her. I recalled all the times we had moved for my husband's career: landing in a new place, miles away from friends and family where I knew literally no one, and unless I could find safe, affordable childcare on the right timeline, there was no way I would be able to continue to work. I never had to fear for my life, and for that I am grateful, but the weight of choose-your-own-adventure childcare was one I knew all too well.

Recall, in the opening of this book I wrote the COVID-19 pandemic cracked open some of society's biggest wounds. Healthcare, racial inequality, and broken leadership are the most frequent headline-makers. But I could now see so clearly the effects of the pandemic could serve to cast a light on our gender-inequities as well—starting with childcare.

In 2017, the Center for American Progress found 42 percent of American children under the age of five live in areas where there is insufficient supply of childcare centers. Supply and demand in the childcare markets was already a problem. Fast forward to 2020 when just about all forms of childcare were forced to shut down either temporarily or permanently, virtually all American parents should be able to relate to Nina's life-altering childcare challenge.[263]

Early numbers are evidence for the dramatic link between access to childcare and maternal workforce participation. An August 2020 federal jobs report showed nearly 1.3 million women aged twenty-five to fifty-four had left the workforce since February of the same year.[264] One out of four women who reported becoming unemployed during the pandemic said it was because of lack of childcare—twice the rate among men.[265]

263 Elissa Strauss, "There's Not Even Close to Enough Child Care in the United States for All the Families That Need It," *Slate*, January 6, 2017.

264 n.a, "Child Care Crisis Pushes US Mothers Out of Labor Force," *Associated Press*, September 5, 2020.

265 Alicia S. Modestino, "Coronovirus child-care will set women back a generation," *Washington Post*, July 29, 2020.

And while it's fun to think everything will go back to "normal" once there's a vaccine, the reality is many childcare centers will close entirely, unable to stay afloat without steady revenue. Previous research shows women who drop out of the workforce for childcare have a harder time re-entering later on, and their overall earnings suffer for the length of their careers.

I could be Nina. You could be Nina. We could all be Nina.

This is where it all comes together for me that consistent childcare is critical to building a healthy society and shouldn't be a result of luck or wealth. And when we write off programs or policies surrounding things like universal childcare, it's a sexist move—plain and simple—because the data shows it will have a deeper impact on women than men. Nina's story pushed me closer to my truth: wanting access to affordable childcare isn't some "socialist bullshit" or "too progressive"—it's a critical piece of the puzzle toward building more gender-equal societies and more equal societies for all. And of course, as I hope you've learned by now, childcare is just one piece of the puzzle. Policies and programs that support economic empowerment, remove gender-bias in education, invest in women's health, and reduce gender-based violence are good for women, but then ultimately are good for all. While the coronavirus pandemic has been devastating on many fronts, it's a chance to push all of us closer to feeling Nina's pain and allow us to see new truths to advocate for real change.

BABOONS: A LESSON IN CHANGE

Never did I ever think apes would make an appearance in a book on gender-equality. Never did I ever think they would make *two* appearances, but here we are. You may recall in the early chapter on matriarchies, I called attention to chimpanzees and bonobos, with whom humans share 99 percent of our DNA, and how chimpanzees have been observed to operate in male-dominant patriarchal structures and bonobos in female-dominant, but ultimately egalitarian, matriarchal structures. I decided to include them in the book because it was an interesting discovery that lent a bit of perspective outside of the human race. But in truth, I didn't think much of it, and I honestly wondered if that section would survive the editing process.

So imagine my surprise when I was reading one of my favorite and most pivotal pieces of research on this journey, *The Double X Economy* by Linda Scott, that she, a woman who was named one of the top twenty-five world thinkers of 2015, was talking about apes in her book too. Scott had gone one step further in her research, however, and provided a tremendous lesson on change.

Scott shares the story of neuroscientist and leading primatologist, Robert Sapolsky. Sapolsky observed a troop of baboons in the savanna of Kenya from 1970 to 1986.[266] Baboons, like chimps, live in a patriarchal structure. Troops operate with a single male at the top who maintains his stature and rank via violence and exploitation of other baboons. Males routinely fight over food, females, territory, and sometimes just for sport. The males are

---

266 Scott, *The Double X,* 96.

organized into stratified ranks beneath the alpha, which dictates which males can terrorize other males, but all males can bully females. This particular troop Sapolsky had been observing was no exception in their behaviors.

The study took a turn in 1986, however, when the top-ranking troop males discovered meat left in the trash at a tourist lodge nearby and consumed it all, predictably refusing to share with lower class males or any of the females. Turns out, the meat was infected with bovine tuberculosis and killed off all of the top males in the troop. The troop that remained was now comprised of a higher percentage population of female baboons and the males who had been living lower on the troop strata.

What happened next is the lesson in change. With the bullies gone, the remaining baboons were higher percentage females and males who Sapolsky had previously observed to be more collaborative. Instead of the next most violent males taking over, "the good guys and the females devised a culture that was less abusive, more cooperative, more egalitarian, and healthier."[267] This culture stuck for the long-haul, with Sapolsky observing even after a decade passed and a complete turnover in the male population of the troop, a more peaceful culture remained. Interestingly enough, it appeared the females ensured the staying power of this more peaceful society by refusing to mate with any males who didn't fall in line with the more peaceful troop philosophy.[268]

As a neuroscientist, Sapolsky's original goals had been to measure stress levels, so he was able to collect and

267 Ibid.

268 Kim Krieger, "A Kinder, Gentler Baboon," AAAS Science, April 13, 2004.

compare health data from the more violent troop of the 1970s to the more peaceful troop of the 1990s. In the early troop, chronic stress was high among females and lower-status males, likely from the everyday threats exacted upon them by the violent males at the top. In the new egalitarian society, however, chronic stress was significantly reduced, and the baboons appeared happier and healthier.[269]

As Scott put so succinctly, "If baboons can change, we can too."[270] We are equipped with far more complex thinking, problem-solving, and change-making skills than our primate relatives. It starts by seeing and understanding the systems of inequality we inherit and perpetuate and committing to build something newer, better, and healthier for us all.

Call it what you will, matriarchy or otherwise, it means no more thug baboons exacting power over others—rather, people of all talents working together harnessing the proven power of inclusion to birth a newer and better way of being for the good of the human race.

I'm game, and I hope you are too.

---

269 Ibid.

270 Scott, *The Double X,* 96.

Acknowledgments

This publishing journey would not have been possible without multiple facets of my life lifting me up and making it possible.

I'm grateful to the Creators Institute for all of the knowledge and guidance provided to me as a member of your December 2020 author's cohort. To all the fellow cohort authors I've met who provided help, encouragement, and camaraderie on this crazy accelerated book-writing journey, thank you. The image of your smiling and supportive faces in Zoom breakout rooms will be forever burned on my brain.

To everyone at New Degree Press who touched this book—both those I'm aware of and those I'm not— thank you. Special thanks to those who spent the most time working with me, my Developmental Editor, Cass Lauer, and my Marketing and Revisions Editor, Natalie Bailey. I would not have made it without both of your partnership and company on the journey. I'll miss our weekly time laughing, working, and dreaming of a better future together. And, to Ashley Lanuza—without your help on citations I'm certain I wouldn't have made my publishing deadline.

Thank you to everyone who contributed to my research and interviews. The time, knowledge, and energy each of you shared has impacted me in a profound and life-changing way. That many of you agreed to connect with me after I reached out randomly is especially humbling and encouraging. I'm energized to know the amazing work you and your organizations are doing empowering women, and I'm humbled you helped make my journey possible.

To my absolutely amazing community of beta readers and supporters, thank you for the outpouring of support you provided to make this book a reality. I cannot begin to convey the joy and delight you provided me on this journey, and in the middle of a tough year. During the crowdfunding campaign especially, seeing the names of new friends, old friends, and complete strangers pop up and support this project was incredibly humbling and gratitude inducing. You all remind me the world is good.

My generous beta-reader community:

Candice Bennett, Eric Cislo, Mike Ahl, Brittany Carpenter, Vicoria McQuade, JoAnn Vroman, Russell Wagner, Erica Anaya, Nicole Craw, Amy Selco, Jessica Shea, Cheryl, Ellsworth, Steven Schooner, Kristin Foti, Joan Wood, John Campbell, Melissa Ferraro, James Cislo, Katie Egger Makris, Ryan Braverman, Marisa Keegan, Diane Lebson, Chris Ian Armstrong, Ana Canning, Kevin and Lauren Curran, Susan Kelly, Richard O Walker III, Mark Swartz, Maria Dunn, MaryAnn Wall, Judy Ahl, Blair Greenbaum, Rebecca Emami, Jim Dahl, Krista Vita, Michele Taylor Fennell, Sarah Parsoneault, Jonina Kelley, Jennifer Jolls, Leiloni Stainsby, Kathy Elcox, Julianne Fisher, Amanda Cole, Melissa Novak, Sarah J. Goggin, Nadine Gabai-Botero, Cass Lauer, Renee Carlineo, Kelly Sorenson, Kelly Quist-Demars, Blake Keegan, Emily McMahan, Meredith Cohen, Nicole Cooley, Rebecca Bryant, Heather A. Lee,

Joy Meadows, Amy Schaffer, Chris Stacey, Allison Brust, Sarah Stanton, Sarah Bass, Angela Bobich, Elizabeth Bennett, Amy DiCapua, Terry Hudson, Jenn Shull, Tanya Jaklis, Alison Fitzgerald, Eric Koester, Matt Lynch, Jodie Sperico, Mike Shethar, Nancy E. Coppola, Tracie Seward, Melissa Bluey, Renee Baruch, Maria Stojanova, Mike Alonzo, Catrina Tangchittsumran, Emma Kieran, Shira Sliffman, Andrea Klein, Courtney Reeve, Stacy Waxler, Christina Cole, Ashlee Droscher, Claire Krawsczyn, Alison Guillaume, Cady North, Scott Pearson, Denise Lane, Lindsey Loyd, Kathleen Schafer, M Clark, Joy Langley, Maria Rauch Baker, Angela Ahl, Derry Deringer, Tee Hutch, Dave Coyne, Sarah Weise, Greg Harding, Laura Khan, Christina Bennett, Tamsin Van Hoozer, Lindsey Lathrop, Jesse Roof, and Evelyn Asher.

To the girlfriends who were there cheering me along and checking in on me in this journey; Britt and Vic, I'd expect nothing less after a lifetime of friendship, but appreciate it that much more because of it. Marisa, your ability to call at just the right moment when I'm struggling is uncanny. This entire book has basically been slow trickled to you via text, and your feedback helped me keep going. Know that each of you and the dreams we have for ourselves and our children are baked into the pages of this book.

To my parents, for all the love and support you gave me growing up that have made me the strong, independent woman I am today. While we may not see eye to eye on the contents of this book and my dreams for the future, you undoubtedly helped me become a person who feels empowered enough to dream big and be heard, and for that I am grateful.

To my brother Dan and his fiancée (maybe now wife) Emily, thank you so much for taking time to read this manuscript cover to cover and providing feedback in the two-week window I requested, at the same time you were buying a house and planning a wedding. That you made time for me and my work during arguably one of the busiest times in your life means so much to me. Your feedback means a great deal to me as well. You pushed me to dig deeper, think bigger, and make changes that undoubtedly made the final product better. I promise to give you the proper hugs you've earned whenever hugging is allowable again.

To my family, Mike, Elizabeth, and Sienna, thank you for enduring all the hours I disappeared to write this book. I wish I had kept better track of all the hours to know just how many it is, but I appreciate your patience with me and any extra tasks you picked up while I was working. You played a huge role in my ability to achieve this goal.

And finally, to the universe. Thanks for putting me in the right place at the right time. For helping me see the silver linings of quarantine during a global pandemic: life slowed down so I could write more and understand how changing the world got a lot more urgent. Keep nudging me, and I'll keep showing up. I promise.

Appendix

_____

INTRODUCTION

"A surprising fact about Feminism." *Chicago Tribune.*
January 7, 2016. https://www.chicagotribune.com/
redeye/redeye-a-surprising-fact-about-feminism-
20160107-story.html

Bartoletti, Susan C. *How Women Won the Vote: Alice Paul, Lucy
Burns, and Their Big Idea.* New York: HarperCollins, 2020.

Ford, Liz. "Nine out of 10 people found to be biased against
women." *The Guardian.* March 5, 2020. https://www.
theguardian.com/global-development/2020/mar/05/
nine-out-of-10-people-found-to-be-biased-against-women

Garrison, Laura T. "6 Modern Societies Where Women Rule."
Mental Floss. March 3, 2017. https://www.mentalfloss.
com/article/31274/6-modern-societies-where-women-
literally-rule

Georgetown Institute for Women, Peace, and Security.
"Women, Peace, and Security Index." Accessed January
31, 2020, https://giwps.georgetown.edu/the-index/

Ghodsee, Kristen R. *Why Women Have Better Sex
Under Socialism: And Other Arguments for Economic
Independence.* New York: Bold Type Books, 2020.

"Kate Sheppard." *Encyclopedia Britannica,* July 9, 2020.
https://www.britannica.com/biography/Kate-Sheppard

Millington, Alison and Erin McDowell. "The 21 best countries in the world to live in if you're a woman." *Business Insider*. August 23, 2019. https://www. businessinsider.com/the-best-countries-for-women-us-news-world-report-2018-3

"Report reveals nearly 90 per cent of all people have 'a deeply ingrained bias' against women." UN News. March 5, 2020. https://news.un.org/en/story/2020/03/1058731.

Rice, Doyle. "The last time the Earth was this warm was 125,000 years ago." *USA Today*. January 18, 2017. https://www.usatoday.com/story/weather/2017/01/18/hottest-year-on-record/96713338/

Ritchie, Hannah, Max Roser, and Esteban Ortiz-Ospina. "Suicide." Our World in Data. 2015. https:// ourworldindata.org/suicide

Scott, Linda. *The Double X Economy: The Epic Potential of Women's Empowerment*. New York City: Farrar, Straus, and Giroux. 2020.

"Tackling Social Norms: a game changer for gender inequalities." Human Development Perspectives. United Nations Development Programs. March 5, 2020. http://hdr.undp.org/sites/default/files/hd_perspectives_gsni.pdf

CHAPTER 1

Debevec, Liza. "Setting the record straight: Matrilineal does not equal matriarchal." Thrive. January 2019. https:// wle.cgiar.org/thrive/2015/10/15/setting-record-straight-matrilineal-does-not-equal-matriarchal

Grady, Constance. "The waves of feminism, and why people keep fighting over them, explained." *Vox.* July 20, 2018. https://www.vox.com/2018/3/20/16955588/feminism-waves-explained-first-second-third-fourth

Merriam-Webster, s.v. "Equality." Accessed July 18, 2020. https://www.merriam-webster.com/dictionary/equality

Merriam-Webster, s.v. "Equity." Accessed October 24, 2020. https://www.merriam-webster.com/dictionary/equity.

Merriam-Webster, s.v. "Inequality." Accessed July 18, 2020. https://www.merriam-webster.com/dictionary/inequality

Merriam-Webster, s.v. "Inequity." Accessed July 18, 2020. *https://www.merriam-webster.com/dictionary/inequity*

Merriam-Webster, s.v. "Matriarchy." Accessed July 18, 2020. https://www.merriam-webster.com/dictionary/matriarchy

Merriam-Webster, s.v. "Patriarchy." Accessed July 18, 2020. https://www.merriam-webster.com/dictionary/patriarchy

CHAPTER 2

Admin. "Bribri; Matriarchy & Feminism Living in CR." *The Costarican Times.* February 20, 2014. https://www.costaricantimes.com/bribri-matriarchy-feminism-living-in-costa-rica/25298

Booth, Hannah. "The kingdom of women: the society where a man is never the boss." *The Guardian.* April 1, 2017.

https://www.theguardian.com/lifeandstyle/2017/apr/01/the-kingdom-of-women-the-tibetan-tribe-where-a-man-is-never-the-boss

Garrison, Laura T. "6 Modern Societies Where Women Rule." Mental Floss. March 3, 2017. https://www.mentalfloss.com/article/31274/6-modern-societies-where-women-literally-rule

Marsden, Harriet. "International Women's Day: What are matriarchies, and where are they now?" Independent. March 08, 2018. https://www.independent.co.uk/news/long_reads/international-womens-day-matriarchy-matriarchal-society-women-feminism-culture-matrilineal-elephant-bonobo-a8243046.html

Mistiaen, Veronique. "Meet the queen mothers: 10,000 amazing women taking back power in Africa." The Telegraph. December 3, 2014. https://www.telegraph.co.uk/women/life/meet-the-queen-mothers-10000-amazing-women-taking-back-power-in/

Ogden, Lesley Evans. "What animals tell us about female leadership." BBC. September 26, 2018. https://www.bbc.com/worklife/article/20180925-with-females-in-charge-bonobo-society-is-more-chilled-out

Oxford Reference, s.v. "Ecofeminism." Accessed January 12, 2020. https://www.oxfordreference.com/view/10.1093/oi/authority.20110803095740943#:~:text=A%20movement%20in%20which%20mankind's,The%20Oxford%20Dictionary%20of%20Philosophy%20%C2%BB

Shapiro, Danielle. "Indonesia's Minangkabau: The World's Largest Matrilineal Society." *The Daily Beast.* July 13, 2017. https://www.thedailybeast.com/indonesias-minangkabau-the-worlds-largest-matrilineal-society?ref=scroll

CHAPTER 3

Cathey, Libby. "Little girls will have to wait 4 more years, Warren says, as 2020 race loses viable female candidates." ABC News. March 8, 2020. https://abcnews.go.com/Politics/persistence-heartbreak-loss-viable-female-candidates-2020-race/story?id=69419365

Connley, Courtney. "Meet Erika James, the first woman to be appointed dean of the Wharton School." CNBC Make It. February 27, 2020. https://www.cnbc.com/2020/02/27/erika-james-becomes-first-female-dean-of-the-wharton-school.html

Domestic Violence. *National Coalition Against Domestic Violence* (n.d.). https://assets.speakcdn.com/assets/2497/domestic_violence-2020080709350855.pdf?1596828650457.

Equal Measures 2030. *2019 Em2030 SDG Gender Index* (2019). https://data.em2030.org/2019-sdg-gender-index/explore-the-2019-index-data/.

Ford, Liz. "Not one single country set to achieve gender equality by 2030." *The Guardian.* June 3, 2019. https://www.theguardian.com/global-development/2019/jun/03/not-one-single-country-set-to-achieve-gender-equality-by-2030

Steinem, Gloria. *Outrageous Acts and Everyday Rebellions.* London: Picador, 2019.

CHAPTER 4

Abouzeid, Rania. "Remaking Rwanda." *National Geographic.* November 2019.

Federal Statistical Office. "Wage gap." Accessed September 22, 2020. https://www.bfs.admin.ch/bfs/en/home/statistics/work-income/wages-income-employment-labour-costs/wage-levels-switzerland/wage-gap.html#3083_1558444685459__content_bfs_en_home_statistiken_arbeit-erwerb_loehne-erwerbseinkommen-arbeitskosten_lohnniveau-schweiz_lohnunterschied_jcr_content_par_tabs

Georgetown Institute for Women, Peace, and Security. *The Dimensions.* Accessed September 22, 2020. https://giwps.georgetown.edu/index-dimensions/

Georgetown Institute for Women, Peace, and Security. *Women, Peace, and Security Index.* Accessed September 22, 2020. https://giwps.georgetown.edu/the-index/

Georgetown Institute for Women, Peace, and Security. *Women, Peace, and Security Index 2019/2020.* Accessed September 22, 2020. https://giwps.georgetown.edu/wp-content/uploads/2019/12/WPS-Index-2019-20-Report.pdf

Hall, Shereen. "How Women Rebuilt Rwanda." *Inclusive Security.* Accessed October 29, 2020. https://www.inclusivesecurity.org/how-women-rebuilt-rwanda/#:~:text=Now%20Available%3A%20Rwandan%20Women%20Rising,lasting%20security%20for%20countries%20worldwide.

Krulwich, Robert. "Non! Nein! No! A Country That Wouldn't Let Women Vote Till 1971." *National Geographic.* August 26, 2016. https://www.nationalgeographic.com/news/2016/08/country-that-didnt-let-women-vote-till-1971/#close

Kurt, Stefanie. "Nation of Brothers with Late Arriving Sisters." NCCR. May 12, 2016. https://blog.nccr-onthemove.ch/nation-of-brothers-with-late-arriving-sisters/

OECD. "Part-time employment rate." Accessed September 22, 2020. https://data.oecd.org/emp/part-time-employment-rate.htm#indicator-chart

Schaverien, Anna and Nick-Cumming Bruce. "Swiss Women Strike Nationwide to Protest Inequalities." *The New York Times.* June 14, 2019. https://www.nytimes.com/2019/06/14/world/europe/switzerland-women-strike.html

Thompson, Georgina. "Sweden, Norway, Iceland, Estonia and Portugal rank highest for family-friendly policies in OECD and EU countries." UNICEF. June 12, 2019. https://www.unicef.org/press-releases/sweden-norway-iceland-and-estonia-rank-highest-family-friendly-policies-oecd-and-eu

Thornton, Alex. "These countries have the most women in parliament." World Economic Forum. February 12, 2019. https://www.weforum.org/agenda/2019/02/chart-of-the-day-these-countries-have-the-most-women-in-parliament/

"Trio of trailblazers: NZ's female Prime Ministers." *Otago Daily Times.* September 19, 2018. https://www.odt.co.nz/news/national/trio-trailblazers-nzs-female-prime-ministers

Warner, Gregory. "It's the No.1 Country for Women
in Politics— But Not in Daily Life." NPR. July
29, 2016. https://www.npr.org/sections/
goatsandsoda/2016/07/29/487360094/invisibilia-no-
one-thought-this-all-womans-debate-team-could-
crush-it

World Economic Forum. *Global Gender Gap Report 2020.*
Accessed September 22, 2020. http://www3.weforum.
org/docs/WEF_GGGR_2020.pdf

"Why gender parity matters." World Economic Forum.
December 19, 2019. https://www.weforum.org/reports/
gender-gap-2020-report-100-years-pay-equality

CHAPTER 5

"Advocates Survey 2018." Equal Measures 2030. Accessed
September 26, 2020. https://www.equalmeasures2030.
org/products/advocate-survey/

Caroli, Daniel. "The Three Biggest Priorities in
Relation to Gender Equality." Tableau Public.
Last modified September 24, 2018. https://public.
tableau.com/profile/daniel.caroli#!/vizhome/
TheThreeBiggestPrioritiesinRelationtoGenderEquality/
Main

Equal Measures 2030. *2019 EM2030 SDG Gender Index.*
Accessed September 26, 2020. https://data.em2030.
org/2019-sdg-gender-index/explore-the-2019-index-data/

Ford, Liz. "Not one single country set to achieve gender
equality by 2030." *The Guardian.* June 3, 2019. https://
www.theguardian.com/global-development/2019/
jun/03/not-one-single-country-set-to-achieve-gender-
equality-by-2030

"Take Action for the Sustainable Development Goals."
United Nations. Accessed September 26, 2020. https://
www.un.org/sustainabledevelopment/sustainable-
development-goals/

"Who We Are." Equal Measures 2030. Accessed September 26,
2020. https://www.equalmeasures2030.org/who-we-are/

CHAPTER 6

Gates, Melinda. *The Moment of Lift: How Empowering Women
Changes the World.* New York: Flatiron Books, 2019.

Kendall, Mikki. *Hood Feminism: Notes from the Women That a
Movement Forgot.* New York: Viking, 2020.

Lovelace, Berkeley Jr. "As U.S. coronavirus deaths cross 100,000,
black Americans bear disproportionate share of fatalities."
CNBC Evolve Spotlight. May 27, 2020. https://www.cnbc.
com/2020/05/27/as-us-coronavirus-deaths-cross-100000
-black-americans-bear-disproportionate-share-of-fatal-
ities.html

Merriam-Webster, s.v. "Intersectionality." Accessed September
26, 2020. https://www.merriam-webster.com/dictionary/
intersectionality

Pay Scale. *The State of the Gender Pay Gap 2020.* Accessed September 26, 2020. https://www.payscale.com/data/gen-
der-pay-gap#section03

CHAPTER 7

Chang, Mariko L. *Shortchanged: Why Women Have Less Wealth
and What Can Be Done About It.* Oxford: Oxford University
Press, 2012.

"Closing the Women's Wealth Gap." *Women's Wealth Gap*. Accessed September 26, 2020. https://womenswealthgap.org/

Edsell, Catherine. "The Matriarch Adventures." *Cathadventure*. Accessed on September 26, 2020. https://cathadventure.com/the-matriarch-adventure

Edsell, Catherine. "How an adventure with other women could change your life." Ted Talks. June 27, 2017. Video, 11:51. https://www.youtube.com/watch?v=kfKB8GAqAGw

Law, Tara. "Women Are Now the Majority of the US Workforce—But Working Women Still Face Serious Challenges." *Time*. January 16, 2020. https://time.com/5766787/women-workforce/

Parker, Kim. "Women more than men adjust their careers for family life." Pew Research Center. October 1, 2015. https://www.pewresearch.org/fact-tank/2015/10/01/women-more-than-men-adjust-their-careers-for-family-life/

Schulte, Brigid. *Overwhelmed: How to Work, Love, and Play When No One Has the Time*. London: Picador, 2015.

Women in the Workplace. *Lean In*. Accessed September 26, 2020. https://wiwreport.s3.amazonaws.com/Women_in_the_Workplace_2019.pdf

CHAPTER 8

Carmon, Irin. "Can American Men and Women Ever Really Be Equal?" *Time*. September 27, 2018. https://time.com/longform/gender-equality-america/

Dishman, Lydia. "What is the glass cliff, and why do so many female CEOs fall off it?" Fast Company. July 27, 2018. https://www.fastcompany.com/90206067/what-is-the-glass-cliff-and-why-do-so-many-female-ceos-fall-off-it

Domonoske, Camila. "Companies in Iceland Now Required to Demonstrate They Pay Men, Women Fairly." NPR The Two Way. January 3, 2018. https://www.npr.org/sections/thetwo-way/2018/01/03/575403863/companies-in-iceland-now-required-to-demonstrate-they-pay-men-women-fairly

Dolan, Kerry A. "The Richest in 2020." *Forbes*. Last modified March 18, 2020. https://www.forbes.com/billionaires/

Henshall, Angela. "What Iceland can teach the world about gender pay gaps." BBC. February 10, 2018. https://www.bbc.com/worklife/article/20180209-what-iceland-can-teach-the-world-about-gender-pay-gaps

Hinchliffe, Emma. "The number of female CEOs in the Fortune 500 hits an all-time record." Fortune. May 18, 2020. https://fortune.com/2020/05/18/women-ceos-fortune-500-2020/

n.a. "America is the only rich country without a law on paid leave for new parents." *The Economist*. July 18, 2019. https://www.economist.com/united-states/2019/07/18/america-is-the-only-rich-country-without-a-law-on-paid-leave-for-new-parents

Pay Scale. *2020 Compensation Best Practices*. Accessed September 27, 2020. https://www.payscale.com/cbpr

"The state of women in corporate America 2019 Report." Lean In. Last modified September 27, 2020. https://leanin.org/women-in-the-workplace-2019

The World Bank. "Benin Receives $90 Million to Invest in Women and Adolescent Girls' Empowerment to Boost its Human Capital." News release. January 25, 2019. The World Bank. Accessed March 21, 2020. https://www.worldbank.org/en/news/press-release/2019/01/25/benin-receives-90-million-to-invest-in-women-and-adolescent-girls-empowerment-to-boost-its-human-capital

Weinberger, Matt and Paige Leskin. "The rise and fall of Marissa Mayer, the once-beloved CEO of Yahoo now pursuing her own venture." Business Insider. February 11, 2020. https://www.businessinsider.com/yahoo-marissa-mayer-rise-and-fall-2017-6

CHAPTER 9

Beck, Julie. "When Sex Ed Discusses Gender Inequality, Sex Gets Safer." The Atlantic. April 27, 2015. https://www.theatlantic.com/health/archive/2015/04/when-sex-ed-teaches-gender-inequality-sex-gets-safer/391460/

Doorways for Women and Families. Accessed September 29, 2020. https://www.doorwaysva.org/

Hattery, Angela J. Gender, Power, and Violence: Responding to Sexual and Intimate Partner Violence in Society Today. Lanham: Rowman & Littlefield Publishers, 2019.

Hood, Katie. "The difference between healthy and unhealthy love." Ted Talks. 2019. Video, 12:06. https://www.ted.com/talks/katie_hood_the_difference_between_healthy_and_unhealthy_love/up-next

Planned Parenthood. "What's the State of Sex Education in the US?" Last accessed September 29, 2020. https://www.plannedparenthood.org/learn/for-educators/whats-state-sex-education-us

RAINN. "The Criminal Justice System: Statistics." Accessed September 29, 2020. https://www.rainn.org/statistics/criminal-justice-system

Rough, Bonnie J. "How the Dutch Do Sex Ed." *The Atlantic.* August 27, 2018. fthhttps://www.theatlantic.com/family/archive/2018/08/the-benefits-of-starting-sex-ed-at-age-4/568225/

One Love. Accessed September 29, 2020. https://www.joinonelove.org/

One Love. "About Yeardley." Accessed September 29, 2020. https://www.joinonelove.org/about-yeardley/

One Love. "Relationships 101." Accessed September 29, 2020. https://www.joinonelove.org/relationships-101/

UN Women. "Facts and Figures: Ending Violence Against Women." Last modified November 2019. https://www.unwomen.org/en/what-we-do/ending-violence-against-women/facts-and-figures

UNICEF. "Behind Closed Doors: The Impact of Domestic Violence on Children." Accessed September 29, 2020.

World Association of Girl Guides and Girl Scouts and UN Women. "Voices Against Violence." UN Women, 2013. https://www.unwomen.org/en/digital-library/publications/2013/10/voices-against-violence-curriculum

CHAPTER 10

AAUW. "Support the Gender Equity in Education Act." Accessed October 3, 2020. https://www.aauw.org/act/two-minute-activist/geea/

Abdelmoneim, David. *No more boys and girls: can our kids go gender free?* BBC. n.d. Video. https://www.bbc.co.uk/programmes/b09202jz

Bailey, Catherine. "No More Boys and Girls? A Series Review About Gender Stereotypes in Schools." Think or Blue. August 21, 2020. https://thinkorblue.com/gender-stereotypes-in-schools/

Bian, Lin, Sarah-Jane Leslie, Andrei Cimpian. "Gender stereotypes about intellectual ability emerge early and influence children's interests." *AAAS Science*, 6323, no. 355 (2017): 389-391. Accessed May 16, 2020. https://science.sciencemag.org/content/355/6323/389

Cimpian, Joseph. "How our education system undermines gender equity." Brookings. April 23, 2018. https://www.brookings.edu/blog/brown-center-chalkboard/2018/04/23/how-our-education-system-undermines-gender-equity/

Pollack, Eileen. "Why are there still so few women in science." *New York Times*. October 6, 2013. https://www.nytimes.com/2013/10/06/magazine/why-are-there-still-so-few-women-in-science.html

"Virginia biochemist is crowned Miss America after performing onstage science experiment." CBS News. December 20, 2019. https://www.cbsnews.com/news/miss-america-2020-virginia-biochemist-camille-schrier-crowned-the-new-miss-america-onstage-science-experiment/

World Economic Forum. "The Future of Jobs Report." Accessed October 3, 2020. http://www3.weforum.org/docs/WEF_Future_of_Jobs_2018.pdf

Strauss, Valerie. "It's 2017, and girls still don't think they are as smart as boys, research shows." *Washington Post.* February 14, 2017. https://www.washingtonpost.com/news/answer-sheet/wp/2017/02/14/its-2017-and-girls-still-dont-think-they-are-as-smart-as-boys-research-shows/

Younger, Jon. "The Future of Work According to WEF Davos 2020: 5 Minute Summary." *Forbes.* February 1, 2020. https://www.forbes.com/sites/jonyounger/2020/02/01/the-future-of-work-according-to-wef-davos-2020-quick-summary/?sh=40042ef25b2c

CHAPTER 11

Atwood, Margaret. *The Handmaid's Tale.* Toronto: McClelland and Stewart, 1985.

Bertakis, Klea D. "Gender Differences in the Utilization of Health Care Services." *J Fam Pract,* 49, no. 2 (2000):147-152. Accessed September 29, 2020. https://www.mdedge.com/familymedicine/article/60747/womens-health/gender-differences-utilization-health-care-services

Boghani, Priyanka. "How Poverty Can Follow Children Into Adulthood." PBS Frontline. November 22, 2017. https://www.pbs.org/wgbh/frontline/article/how-poverty-can-follow-children-into-adulthood/

Centers for Disease Control and Prevention. "Births and Natality." Last modified January 20, 2017. https://www.cdc.gov/nchs/fastats/births.htm

Centers for Disease Control and Prevention. "Depression Among Women." Last modified May 14, 2020. https://www.cdc.gov/reproductivehealth/depression/index.htm

Centers for Disease Control and Prevention. "Leading
    Causes of Death—Females—All races and origins—
    United States, 2017." Last modified November 20, 2019.
    https://www.cdc.gov/women/lcod/2017/all-races-
    origins/index.htm

Clack, Zoanne. "Women's health concerns are dismissed
    more, studied less." *National Geographic.* December
    17, 2019. https://www.nationalgeographic.com/
    magazine/2020/01/womens-health-concerns-are-
    dismissed-more-studied-less-feature/

Duffin, Erin. "Birth rate by family income in the U.S. 2017."
    Statista. July 16, 2020. https://www.statista.com/
    statistics/241530/birth-rate-by-family-income-in-
    the-us/

Family Violence Prevention and Services Program. "The
    Affordable Care Act and Women's Health." Last modified
    December 2013. https://www.acf.hhs.gov/sites/default/
    files/fysb/aca_fvpsa_20131211.pdf

Finlayson, Kenneth. "What matters to women in the
    postnatal period: A meta-synthesis of qualitative
    studies." *PLoS ONE,* 15, no. 4 (2020): e0231415. https://doi.
    org/10.1371/journal.pone.0231415.

Flynn, Andrea. "The Economic Case for Funding Planned
    Parenthood." *The Atlantic.* September 17, 2015. https://
    www.theatlantic.com/business/archive/2015/09/
    planned-parenthood-economic-benefits/405922/

Goodwin, Joanne L. "Mothers' Pensions." *Encyclopedia of
    Chicago.* Last accessed September 29, 2020. http://www.
    encyclopedia.chicagohistory.org/pages/845.html

"How do countries fight falling birth rates?" BBC News.
January 15, 2020. https://www.bbc.com/news/world-
europe-51118616

Khazan, Olga. "The High Cost of Having a Baby in America."
The Atlantic. January 6, 2020. https://www.theatlantic.
com/health/archive/2020/01/how-much-does-it-cost-
have-baby-us/604519/

Lino, Mark. "The Cost of Raising a Child." US Department of
Agriculture. February 18, 2020. https://www.usda.gov/
media/blog/2017/01/13/cost-raising-child

Macrotrends. "Sweden Fertility Rate 1950-2020."
Accessed September 29, 2020. https://www.
macrotrends.net/countries/SWE/sweden/fertility-
rate#:~:text=Sweden%20-%20Historical%20
Fertility%20Rate%20Data%20%20,%20%20
-0.590%25%20%2067%20more%20rows%20

Macrotrends. "US Fertility Rate 1950-2020." Accessed
September 29, 2020. https://www.macrotrends.net/
countries/USA/united-states/fertility-rate

Maternal Health Task Force. "Maternal Health in the United
States." Accessed September 29, 2020. https://www.
mhtf.org/topics/maternal-health-in-the-united-states/

Partnership for Maternal, Newborn, and Child Health.
"The Economic Benefits of Investing in Women's and
Children's Health." Last modified 2013. https://www.
who.int/pmnch/knowledge/publications/summaries/
knowledge_summaries_24_economic_case/en/

Sandhu, Serina. "Mothers 'should be given £2,000 pension top-up for having to take time off work to have children'." INews. June 3, 2019, last modified October 8, 2020. https://inews.co.uk/news/pension-penalty-government-give-mothers-2000-top-up-which-297433

Stengel, Geri. "Market Ripe for Disruption Lacks Investment." *Forbes.* July 8, 2020. https://www.forbes.com/sites/geristengel/2020/07/08/womens-healthcare-a-market-ripe-for-disruption/#1d1a9a5c1a01

World Health Organization. "Ten top issues for women's health." Accessed September 29, 2020. https://www.who.int/life-course/news/commentaries/2015-intl-womens-day/en/

World Population Review. "Total Fertility Rate 2020." Accessed September 29, 2020. https://worldpopulationreview.com/country-rankings/total-fertility-rate

CHAPTER 12

Basu, Zachary. "52 percent of Americans would feel "very comfortable" with a female president." Axios. November 27, 2018. https://www.axios.com/poll-americans-comfortable-female-president-world-af57cdde-4e40-4deb-9855-9f86453ad99b.html

Bowden, Ebony. "Barack Obama says world would be a better place if run by women." *New York Post.* December 16, 2019. https://nypost.com/2019/12/16/barack-obama-says-world-would-be-a-better-place-if-run-by-women/

Chamorro-Premuzic, Tomas. "Are Women Better At Managing The Covid19 Pandemic?" *Forbes.* April 10, 2020. https://www.forbes.com/sites/tomaspremuzic/2020/04/10/are-female-leaders-better-at-managing-the-covid19-pandemic/?sh=5cb7073a28d4

Chamorro-Premuzic, Tomas. "Why Do So Many Incompetent Men Become Leaders?" *Harvard Business Review*. August 22, 2013. https://hbr.org/2013/08/why-do-so-many-incompetent-men

Council on Foreign Relations. "Women's Power Index." Last modified September 18, 2020. https://www.cfr.org/article/womens-power-index

Fifield, Anna. "New Zealand Isn't Just Flattening the Curve, It's Squashing It." *Washington Post*. April 7, 2020. https://www.washingtonpost.com/world/asia_pacific/new-zealand-isnt-just-flattening-the-curve-its-squashing-it/2020/04/07/6cab3a4a-7822-11ea-a311-adb1344719a9_story.html

Fincher, Leta H. "Women leaders are doing a disproportionately great job at handling the pandemic. So why aren't there more of them?" CNN. April 16, 2020. https://www.cnn.com/2020/04/14/asia/women-government-leaders-coronavirus-hnk-intl/index.html

Georgetown Institute for Women, Peace, and Security. *Women, Peace, and Security Index 2019/2020.* Accessed October 3, 2020. http://giwps.georgetown.edu/wp-content/uploads/2019/10/WPS-Index-2019-Data.xlsx

Haynes, Suyin. "Female 2020 Democratic Presidential Candidates Face a 'Gender Penalty' Online, Study Finds." *Time*. November 5, 2019. https://time.com/5717376/female-democratic-candidates-2020-twitter-study/

Henley, Jon and Eleanor A. Roy. "Are female leaders more successful at managing the coronavirus crisis?" The Guardian, April 25, 2020. https://www.theguardian.com/

world/2020/apr/25/why-do-female-leaders-seem-to-be-more-successful-at-managing-the-coronavirus-crisis

Hollingsworth, Julia. "How New Zealand went 100 days with no community coronavirus transmission." CNN. August 10, 2020. https://www.cnn.com/2020/08/10/asia/new-zealand-coronavirus-milestone-intl-hnk-scli/index.html

IPU Parline." Monthly ranking of women in national parliaments." Last modified October 1, 2020. https://data.ipu.org/women-ranking?month=10&year=2020

Knisely, Amelia F. "Teen girls are missing school because they don't have access to feminine hygiene products." *Tennessean*. August 14, 2018. https://www.tennessean.com/story/news/education/2018/08/14/lack-feminine-hygiene-products-keeps-girls-out-school/948313002/

McCartney, Robert. "Virgina's Year of the Woman produces historic package of liberal legislation." *Washington Post*. March 1, 2020. https://www.washingtonpost.com/local/virginia-politics/virginias-year-of-the-woman-produces-historic-package-of-liberal-legislation/2020/03/01/4d1177da-599b-11ea-ab68-101ecfec2532_story.html

Meredith, Sam. "Belarus' president dismisses coronavirus risk, encourages citizens to drink vodka and visit saunas." CNBC. March 31, 2020. https://www.cnbc.com/2020/03/31/coronavirus-belarus-urges-citizens-to-drink-vodka-visit-saunas.html

Merriam-Webster, s.v. "Leadership." Accessed October 3, 2020. https://www.merriam-webster.com/dictionary/leadership.

Michelson, Joan. "What's the Surprising Leadership Lesson in The COVID-19 Crisis?" *Forbes.* March 28, 2020. https://www.forbes.com/sites/joanmichelson2/2020/03/28/whats-the-surprising-leadership-lesson-in-the-covid-19-crisis/?sh=3e76d2a449b6

Ng, Edwin and Carles Muntaner. "The more women in government, the healthier a population." The Conversation. January 9, 2019. https://theconversation.com/the-more-women-in-government-the-healthier-a-population-107075

The National WWII Museum. "History At a Glance: Women in World War II." Accessed December 6, 2020, https://www.nationalww2museum.org/students-teachers/student-resources/research-starters/women-wwii

Tortoriello, Nicole. "Four major wins for gender equity in Virginia's 2020 legislative session." ACLU Virginia. May 8, 2020. https://acluva.org/en/news/four-major-wins-gender-equity-virginias-2020-legislative-session

Valenti, Jessica. "The VP Candidate Isn't Being Vetted. She's Being Scrutinized." *Medium.* August 4, 2020. https://gen.medium.com/the-vp-candidate-isnt-being-vetted-she-s-being-scrutinized-60d0218f6c28

Worldometer. "COVID-19 Coronavirus Pandemic Live Update." Last updated November 16, 2020. https://www.worldometers.info/coronavirus/#countries

CHAPTER 13

American Psychological Association. "Gender and Stress." News release. Last modified 2012. American Psychological Association. Accessed September 19, 2020.

https://www.apa.org/news/press/releases/stress/2010/
gender-stress#:~:text=Women%20are%20more%20
likely%20than%20men%20(28%20percent%20
vs.,10%20(39%20percent)%20men.

Amiel, Sandrine. "Women in Science: Five countries
    that beat the gender gap." Euronews. Last modified
    November 2, 2019. https://www.euronews.
    com/2019/02/11/women-in-science-five-countries-that-
    beat-the-gender-gap

Carmon, Irin. "Can American Men and Women Ever Really
    Be Equal?" *Time*. September 27, 2020. https://time.com/
    longform/gender-equality-america/

Gallup. "Gallup 2019 Global Emotions Report." Accessed
    October 4, 2020. https://www.gallup.com/
    analytics/248906/gallup-global-emotions-report-2019.
    aspx

Martela, Frank et. al. "The Nordic Exceptionalism: What
    Explains Why the Nordic Countries Are Constantly
    Among the Happiest in the World." World Happiness
    Report. March 20, 2020. https://worldhappiness.report/
    ed/2020/the-nordic-exceptionalism-what-explains-
    why-the-nordic-countries-are-constantly-among-the-
    happiest-in-the-world/

Merriam-Webster, s.v. "Freedom." Accessed October 6,
    2020. https://www.merriam-webster.com/dictionary/
    freedom

Partanen, Anu. *The Nordic Theory of Everything: In Search of
    a Better Life.* New York: Harper Paperbacks, 2017.

Solly, Meilan. "Americans Are Among the Most Stressed-Out People in the World, Reporting Negative Emotions at Highest Rates in a December ade." *Smithsonian Magazine.* April 26, 2019. https://www.smithsonianmag.com/smart-news/americans-are-some-most-stressed-out-people-world-reporting-negative-emotions-highest-rates-December ade-180972047/

CHAPTER 14

Day, Meagan. "The story of the Equal Rights Amendment and the woman who killed it." *Medium.* September 7, 2016. https://timeline.com/equal-rights-amendment-schlafly-5567aa191067

Domonoske, Camila. "Companies In Iceland Now Required To Demonstrate They Pay Men, Women Fairly." NPR. January 3, 2018. https://www.npr.org/sections/thetwo-way/2018/01/03/575403863/companies-in-iceland-now-required-to-demonstrate-they-pay-men-women-fairly

Esfandiari, Haleh. "The Women's Movement." The Iran Primer. October 6, 2010. https://iranprimer.usip.org/resource/womens-movement#:~:text=Iranian%20women%20made%20considerable%20progress,vote%20and%20run%20for%20parliament

Georgetown Institute for Women, Peace, and Security. *Women, Peace, and Security Index 2017/2018.* Accessed October 10, 2020. https://giwps.georgetown.edu/wp-content/uploads/2019/11/WPS-Index-Report-2017-18.pdf

Government of Iceland. "Equal Pay Certification." Accessed October 10, 2020. https://www.government.is/topics/human-rights-and-equality/equal-pay-certification/

Grady, Constance. « The waves of feminism, and why people keep fighting over them, explained." *Vox*. July 20, 2018. https://www.vox.com/2018/3/20/16955588/feminism-waves-explained-first-second-third-fourth

Halperin, Anna. "Richard Nixon bears responsibility for the pandemic's child-care crisis." *Washington Post*. August 6, 2020. https://www.washingtonpost.com/outlook/2020/08/06/richard-nixon-bears-responsibility-pandemics-child-care-crisis/

Hutzler, Alexandra. "These Are All The States That Have Passed Anti-Abortion Laws in 2019." Newsweek. May 31, 2019. https://www.newsweek.com/state-abortion-laws-2019-list-1440609

n.a. "Iranian women—before and after the Islamic Revolution." BBC. February 8, 2019. https://www.bbc.com/news/world-middle-east-47032829

Merriam-Webster, s.v. "Brain Drain." Accessed October 10, 2020, https://www.merriam-webster.com/dictionary/brain%20drain

Milligan, Susan. "Stepping Through History." US News. January 20, 2017. https://www.usnews.com/news/the-report/articles/2017-01-20/timeline-the-womens-rights-movement-in-the-us

Save the Children. "The Urban Disadvantage 2015 Report." Accessed October 10, 2020.

Zoellner, Danielle. "Five major things Trump has done to roll back women's rights." *Independent*. March 6, 2020. https://www.independent.co.uk/news/world/americas/us-politics/trump-women-international-womens-day-abortion-policies-healthcare-a9380411.html

CHAPTER 15

Cooper, Marianne. "Mothers' Careers Are at Extraordinary Risk Right Now." *The Atlantic*. October 1, 2020. https://www.theatlantic.com/family/archive/2020/10/pandemic-amplifying-bias-against-working-mothers/616565/

Generation Equality. "Women Deliver." Accessed October 11, 2020. https://generationequality.womendeliver.org/

Merriam-Webster, s.v. "Empowerment." Accessed September 26, 2020. https://www.merriam-webster.com/dictionary/empowerment

McKinsey & Company. "Women in the Workplace 2020." Accessed October 11, 2020. https://wiw-report.s3.amazonaws.com/Women_in_the_Workplace_2020.pdf

Roy, Katica. "Here's how to achieve gender equality after the pandemic." World Economic Forum. April 25, 2020. https://www.weforum.org/agenda/2020/04/how-to-achieve-gender-equality-after-pandemic/

Williams, Joan C. "The Pandemic Has Exposed the Fallacy of the "Ideal Worker." *Harvard Business Review*. May 11, 2020. https://hbr.org/2020/05/the-pandemic-has-exposed-the-fallacy-of-the-ideal-worker

CHAPTER 16

Krieger, Kim. "A Kinder, Gentler Baboon." *AAAS Science*. April 13, 2004. https://www.sciencemag.org/news/2004/04/kinder-gentler-baboon

n.a. "Child Care Crisis Pushes US Mothers Out of Labor Force." *Associated Press.* September 5, 2020. https://www.voanews.com/economy-business/child-care-crisis-pushes-us-mothers-out-labor-force

Modestino, Alicia S. "Coronovirus child-care will set women back a generation." *Washington Post.* July 29, 2020. https://www.washingtonpost.com/us-policy/2020/07/29/childcare-remote-learning-women-employment/

Strauss, Elissa. "There's Not Even Close to Enough Child Care in the United States for All the Families That Need It." *Slate.* January 6, 2017. https://slate.com/human-interest/2017/01/theres-not-enough-child-care-in-the-u-s-for-all-the-families-that-need-it.html

CPSIA information can be obtained
at www.ICGtesting.com
Printed in the USA
FSHW021900080121
77518FS

9 781636 766072